THE END OF
SPECTATOR
CHURCH

Shippensburg, PA

ANSWERING GOD'S
CALL TO FULL ENGAGEMENT

THE END OF
SPECTATOR
CHURCH

TONY COOKE

Published by Harrison House Publishers
Shippensburg, PA 17257

ISBN 13 TP: 978-1-6675-0008-9

ISBN 13 eBook: 978-1-6675-0009-6

For Worldwide Distribution, Printed in the U.S.A.

1 2 3 4 5 6 7 8 / 27 26 25 24 23

So now, if you love the Lord, if you have only just believed in him, begin to do something for him at once. It is a pity that we have so many Christian people, so-called, who do nothing for Christ, literally nothing. He dies for them, redeems them with his precious blood, and they have done nothing for him in return. We need to have a Church in which all the members do something, in which all do all they can, in which all are always doing all they can; for this is what our Lord deserves to have from a living, loving people bought with His precious blood! If He has saved me, I will serve Him forever and ever. And whatever lies in my power to do for His glory, that shall be my delight to do, and to do at once!

—Charles Spurgeon[1]

CONTENTS

ABOUT THE COVER

Did you notice the empty seats on the cover of this book? Did they strike you a certain way? Evoke any emotions in you? As a Bible teacher, I regret seeing empty seats in a church sanctuary because I know how much people could benefit—both eternally and temporally—by being in the room. Steve Smothermon, a pastor friend of mine in New Mexico, has a sign in his church building that says, "An empty seat is a serious matter." Really, all preachers who care about people want to see the seats filled. They especially pray that the lost and those far from God will be there. They want them to hear God's Word and learn about his love so that their lives can be changed.

Another pastor friend, Norm Dubois in Florida, has a sign in his office that reads, "As long as heaven and hell are a reality, church growth is not an option." These kinds of sentiments are very sobering to me, and I hope they are to you as well. Of course, we want people to come to gatherings where worship and proclamation occur because we recognize the life-transforming benefits. We need to worship with those of like precious faith, fellowship with other believers, hear God's Word, and (especially) be equipped and mobilized to serve others.

When I saw those empty seats and chose this picture for the cover, it wasn't because I want auditoriums to be empty. Heavens, no! Rather,

I want the readers to understand that just sitting in meetings is not the sum and substance of our faith; neither is it the end goal of the Christian life. Perhaps we can see these empty seats in a more positive light than described above. Maybe we can understand that once people have been enriched and equipped after sitting in such seats, they leave them to go and do something significant for the Kingdom of God.

I remember once seeing a sign above the back doors of a sanctuary—words you couldn't miss as you exited. The sign read, "The worship is over. The service is just beginning." In another location, I saw signs posted so that drivers exiting the church property could take in the message: "You are now entering the mission field." These sayings capture the true intent of this book.

Of course, I want you to sit under the teaching of God's Word in a great church, but I want you to know that church is not ultimately about passively observing or casually spectating. Jesus prayed for laborers (see Matthew 9:38). My prayer is that all you receive from being in great services and all that you derive from this book will take you far beyond being a spectator, that it will mobilize, activate, propel, and energize you and countless others into the greatest adventure of all—serving God and others with all of our hearts.

INTRODUCTION

I should probably 'fess up at the very beginning of this book. I grew up as a church spectator, a mere observer. In the traditional church where I attended, it never occurred to me that there was any way to be involved except for the occasional rotation of being a greeter. Individuals would sign up to stand in the lobby, welcome people to the service, and give them a bulletin. I did that once in my teenage years. I'm sure there were several areas where people were involved, but I was oblivious to them. Come to think of it, there was the choir, but I was not inclined to singing, so that was not an option. I was basically a pew-sitter and was very content in that role.

Beyond those few volunteer functions, I knew about the pastor, the clergyman, the preacher. He was God's man. He was in a totally different class from me as a commoner. I guess I somewhat revered him, assuming he had some kind of connection with God that I did not have, but I remember thinking preaching was not a desirable task. Around eighth grade, I was feeling terrified while riding a roller coaster for the first time, and in overwhelming fear, I silently prayed, "God, if you get me off of this thing, I'll become a preacher." As soon as I got off the roller coaster, I hoped that God understood I really only said that under duress.

While I respected God, the Bible, and church, the services were not something I really enjoyed. As an even younger child, I remember telling my parents that church was boring and that I didn't understand what was being said. On a few occasions, I got out of Sunday morning services by claiming to have a stomachache. They quickly caught on when they realized I was perfectly fine all-day Saturday and would recover remarkably just in time to go out and play with friends on Sunday afternoon. The effectiveness of that ruse was very short lived.

In the summer after my third-grade year, I actually became a fugitive from Vacation Bible School. I greatly resisted the idea of going to church all week long (playing with neighborhood friends was much more fun), but my mom forced me to go to VBS anyway. She acquiesced when I asked her not to accompany me into the building to register. However, she did not anticipate that I would stand inside the door until she drove off and then escape to a nearby shopping center and spend a few hours killing time before walking a couple of miles down Highway 22 back to my house outside the city limits.

My mom was confused and suspicious when I showed up at home unexpectedly, so I explained to her that VBS had let out early and that another parent had driven me home. That feeble falsehood was hardly convincing, and when she called the church and discovered I had not even registered, I was totally busted. The next day, I received a personal escort into the building and into the classroom. I won't bother giving the details of the time during early middle school when I hid for a couple of hours in the very top of a linen closet to avoid having to attend a youth event at church on Sunday evening.

When I was growing up, children sat with their parents during the adult Sunday morning service. There were no high-energy, entertaining programs for kids, but I did get to use a very small pencil and draw pictures on the back of the bulletin. Batman and guns were favorite themes in my artwork, and that helped a little bit in passing the time.

Though I was often unengaged in the church services, there were still definite benefits to being there. At the time, I didn't consider church exciting or fun, but I am now thankful that I heard and became acquainted with some very powerful truths. I learned about the Ten Commandments and the Sermon on the Mount. Weekly, we recited the Lord's Prayer and the Apostles' Creed, and some of the hymns impacted me in ways I did not appreciate at that time. I am deeply thankful for all of those. Still, I don't recall ever being encouraged to serve or get involved. Perhaps that was mentioned, and I was just not listening. To me, *church* simply meant attending a service and going through the motions. I was primarily a spectator.

As an adult, I now realize there were a couple of times when a particular Scripture was read in church, and it made a significant impression on my life. In spite of the fact that I was not thrilled to be there, the Holy Spirit still, on occasion, took something that was said and branded that truth in my heart. I'm saying all of this to communicate that being a spectator in church can still yield some rich benefits. Though God has more for us than that, I am truly grateful and appreciative whenever people put themselves in a place where they can honor him, receive his Word, and be around his people.

Maybe in that sense we all need to "spectate" some, but hopefully we won't stop there. Early in Jesus' ministry, we twice encounter the phrase, *"Come and see"* (John 1:39, 46). Andrew and Nathaniel were the ones to whom that phrase was directed, and they certainly spectated for a while. But while they were with Jesus, they were being taught and ultimately became highly engaged and active in serving God.

Watching, listening, and learning in church is not an end in and of itself; it should be a launching pad into active engagement and vibrant service. I understand that many will come to a church service just to check things out and see what it's all about. We celebrate such exploration, but we can also pray that such inquirers will eventually become engaged with God and the Body of Christ in profound and meaningful ways.

As you read this book, I pray that your heart will awaken to the fullness of God's destiny for your life. He has a plan and a purpose for you. He wants you to receive abundantly, but he also greatly desires that much will flow through you toward others. My great desire is that you will locate yourself in the following chapters, that you will discover the graces, gifts, and potential that God has placed within you, and that you will experience the overwhelming fulfillment and gratitude that comes from doing what you were born to do. With this in mind, let's explore how we can put an end to church that *merely* involves spectating and discover how God so greatly desires to mobilize and empower you and all of his people in these last days.

Before we jump into the first chapter, let me share an illustration that will set the stage for the mentality we are seeking to promote through this book.

CRUISE SHIP OR BATTLESHIP?

Have you ever heard someone yell, "All hands on deck"? What about, "All hands to battle stations"? Such urgent pleas will be heard on a battleship during a time of war. You will not hear such phrases on a pleasure cruise in the Caribbean or the Mediterranean.

My dad was assigned to an escort ship during World War II in the Pacific. Specifically, they accompanied other ships that had been damaged to get repaired so they could re-engage in the war effort. The sailors understood that they were on a mission and that they were serving a purpose bigger than themselves. Everyone on that ship had duties and responsibilities; no one was there for their personal comfort, ease, or enjoyment.

How different that is from a cruise ship where the passengers are merely on board for fun and relaxation. People who go on cruises are looking to get away from responsibilities, not to embrace them. It is enjoyable to have someone clean and make up your room, provide fun and entertainment for you, take you to exotic and beautiful locations, and cook all of your meals. Did I mention that many "cruisers" will gain seven pounds on a seven-day cruise?

I am not trying to make anyone feel guilty if they have the opportunity to enjoy a pleasure cruise. I have gone on a few, and they are fun. My desire, though, is for believers to consider their overall view of what church is about. Is church supposed to be like a cruise ship where everyone comes to be catered to and to seek their personal enjoyment? Or is church more like a battleship where we all have responsibilities, we all contribute, and we all are living for a purpose bigger than ourselves? Thankfully, Scripture makes this abundantly clear.

CHAPTER ONE

EVERYTHING CHANGED

"Pentecost isn't over yet!"
—D. L. Moody

In the Old Testament, God's people were spectators in certain ways. The priests interacted with God on behalf of the people. The "holy men" were mediators who received offerings from the people and made sacrifices to God on their behalf. The people kept their distance; they understood that only the priests could perform those duties and go into God's presence. To put it simply, there was a sharp and radical distinction between the professionals or *clergy* (to borrow a more modern term) and the *laity*, the common people.

Similarly, the prophets spoke to the people on God's behalf. The people did not enjoy the personal sense of righteousness that we now have through the blood of the Lord Jesus Christ, nor did they have the Holy Spirit—the Comforter—living on the inside of them. God spoke of a better day, in the future, when he stated, *"…I will put My law in their minds, and write it on their hearts; and I will be their God, and they shall be My people"* (Jeremiah 31:33 NKJV). But at that time, a considerable gap remained.

We see this chasm between God and the common people vividly illustrated when Moses received the Law from God. The Lord had said that the people of Israel were to be *"my kingdom of priests, my holy nation"* (Exodus 19:6 NLT), but at that time the people could not handle it.

Moses led them out from the camp to meet with God, and they stood at the foot of the mountain.... When the people heard the thunder and the loud blast of the ram's horn, and when they saw the flashes of lightning and the smoke billowing from the mountain, they stood at a distance, trembling with fear. And they said to Moses, "You speak to us, and we will listen. But don't let God speak directly to us, or we will die!" (Exodus 19:17; 20:18–19 NLT).

After this, in Exodus 28, God established the Levitical priesthood. Aaron and his sons would serve as priests or intermediaries on behalf of the people. Other members of the tribe to which Aaron belonged—the Levites—would assist the priests with various duties around the Tabernacle and later the Temple. These were the sacred places where sacrifice and worship took place. Only the priests would draw near to God, while the common people, the non-priests, kept their distance. That was the system then—under that covenant—but it is not how things are today.

Jesus' blood changed everything.

The Savior's death, burial, and resurrection changed everything.

The New Birth changed everything.

The outpouring of the Holy Spirit on the day of Pentecost changed everything.

While the people in the Old Testament were terrified at the manifestation of God's awesomeness and holiness, Hebrews 10:22 admonishes today's believer, *"Let us draw near with a true heart in full assurance of faith, having our hearts sprinkled from an evil conscience and our bodies washed with pure water"* (NKJV). The common people in the Old Testament pulled back from God's presence, but we—all born-again children of God—are able to draw near because of what Jesus has done for us.

EVERYBODY

While the Old Testament system allowed only a select few to be priests, Peter wrote to multiple congregations of believers and told them all—every one of them—that they were *"a chosen generation, a royal priesthood, a holy nation, His own special people"* (1 Peter 2:9 NKJV). It is difficult to overstate the radical, revolutionary transformation that took place with the coming of the Holy Spirit, but Joel had prophesied centuries before what would happen (see Joel 2:28–29). Recognizing the monumental nature of the moment, Peter quoted Joel, the Old Testament prophet, in his message following the outpouring of the Holy Spirit.

> *This is the fulfillment of what was prophesied through the prophet Joel, for God says: 'This is what I will do in the last days—I will pour out my Spirit on everybody and cause your sons and daughters to prophesy, and your young men will see visions, and your old men will experience dreams from God. The Holy Spirit will come upon all my servants, men and women alike, and they will prophesy* (Acts 2:16–18 TPT).

Many modern Christians have heard Joel's prophecy and Peter's reiteration of it so frequently that they simply take it for granted, but this marked an extreme shift among those who heard it on the streets of Jerusalem nearly two thousand years ago. No longer would it be only the prophet, priest, and king who were anointed by the Spirit. The veil of the Temple had been torn right down the middle at the time of Jesus' crucifixion (see Matthew 27:51), and we all beheld a new *"great High Priest"* (Hebrews 4:14 NKJV) through whom we approach God. Paul taught that *"there is one God and one Mediator between God and men, the Man Christ Jesus"* (1 Timothy 2:5 NKJV). No longer would Aaron and his male descendants be the mediators between God and his people.

When Peter quoted Joel, the outpouring of the Spirit that Peter ref-erenced had just occurred at the beginning of the same chapter—Acts 2. Luke, the author of Acts, went out of his way to emphasize that this experience—the infilling of the Holy Spirit—was for every believer.

> **All the believers** [120 in number] *were meeting together in one place* (Acts 2:1 NLT).

> *What looked like flames or tongues of fire appeared and settled on* **each of them** (Acts 2:3 NLT).

> **They were all filled** *with the Holy Spirit and began to speak with other tongues, as the Spirit gave them utterance* (Acts 2:4 NKJV).

Did you notice the inclusivity of this experience? *"All the believers"; "each of them"; "they were all filled."* This was not just for the twelve or some exceptional, holy, particular priestly class. It was for every believer. God excluded none of those that were trusting in him.

When we examine Joel's prophecy (which Peter quoted), we see this emphasis upon every believer's participation and involvement; no one is omitted. Consider again these phrases from Acts 2:17–18:

> *...I will pour out my Spirit on* **everybody** *and cause your* **sons and daughters** *to prophesy...* (Acts 2:17 TPT).

> *...Your* **young men** *will see visions, and your* **old men** *will experience dreams from God* (Acts 2:17 TPT).

> *The Holy Spirit will come upon* **all my servants, men and women alike,** *and they will prophesy* (Acts 2:18 TPT).

If you have ever felt that the ministry was someone else's responsibility, please think again! We are not all called to be preachers in the traditional sense, but it is God's plan that we all be impacted by and give an expression of his Spirit to others. The time for believers to be mere spectators and observers concerning the things of God ended two thousand years ago.

The resurrection of Jesus and the outpouring of the Holy Spirit broke all of the barriers and all of the walls that separated his covenant people. Today's word is *everybody*! If you are young or old, a son or daughter, a man or a woman, God has a plan and a purpose for your life. You—along with every other believer—comprise the Temple of the Holy Spirit. Paul asked believers, *"Don't you realize that all of you together are the temple of God and that the Spirit of God lives in you?"* (1 Corinthians 3:16 NLT). We are all a part, and we are all vitally connected to God and to one another through the New Birth and the communion of the Holy Spirit.

INFLUENCE AND EXPRESSION

In addition to the theme of *everybody* in Acts 2:17–18, we should recognize the idea of God's *influence*—that God pours out his Spirit upon *all* of his children, not just on a select few or a special class as it had been under the previous covenant. This influence of God's Spirit comes to produce an *expression*. For example, Joel and Peter both said that when the Spirit came upon God's servants, they would prophesy. In other words, God would put something on the inside of them so that something could come forth on the outside.

Please don't fail to recognize the radical and revolutionary significance of Joel's prophecy, as well as its fulfillment on the day of Pentecost in Acts 2. An absolutely new paradigm was established. Barriers that had existed for centuries were demolished. People no longer had to go through an earthly mediator to access God. It was no longer just the prophet, priest, and king who would be empowered by the Holy Spirit. It was no longer just the wise, old sage who could speak on God's behalf. God's Spirit was now to be poured out upon all flesh—young and old, male and female. Receiving and expressing God's influence was no longer a spectator sport for the vast majority. Everyone was invited on the field to play!

WHAT JOEL DID NOT SEE

As powerful as Joel's prophesy was, it was limited in its scope. Prophets are not omniscient, and they only know what the Lord specifically reveals to them. Usually that is quite partial in nature. Paul wrote to the Corinthians, *"Our knowledge is partial and incomplete, and even the gift of prophecy reveals only part of the whole picture!"* (1 Corinthians 13:9 NLT). What we will soon discover is that while Joel's prophecy was one hundred percent accurate, it would later be amplified and expanded upon, especially as the era of the church began.

This brings us to the term *progressive revelation,* which is very important when it comes to properly interpreting the Bible. This means that God typically reveals things to humanity piece by piece and part by part. Its natural correlation would be that when an elementary student is introduced to math, the teacher doesn't start with algebra and calculus. Rather, the teacher will start by teaching the student what the numbers are, and then move to addition, subtraction, and so forth. A wise teacher knows that learning must be progressive, that building blocks of understanding must be laid before they can be built upon.

Likewise, God reveals truth to humanity gradually and progressively. In the Old Testament, for example, certain foundational truths are hinted at and partially revealed, and as time progresses, more is revealed. For example, in the early part of Genesis, God's ultimate redemptive plan is suggested through the promised seed (offspring) of the woman, who would crush the head of the serpent (see Genesis 3:15), and through the shedding of blood when God made coats of skin and covered the nakedness of Adam and Eve (see Genesis 3:21). However, these early projections were significantly amplified and clarified throughout time. Not only did later Old Testament prophecies provide more details (looking forward), but much greater clarity emerged when Jesus came as the Ultimate Sacrifice, and his redemptive work was further expounded upon through New Testament writings such as Romans and Hebrews (looking back at the cross).

Another way to illustrate progressive revelation is to imagine being in a dark room. If the door is opened just a few inches and the light is on in the hallway, some of that light comes in and begins to illuminate objects in the room. You may not be able to make them out distinctly because the door is only open a couple of inches. However, as the door progressively opens wider and wider, and more light floods into the room, the objects become clear and distinct, and colors become more vibrant and distinguishable.

Even though Jesus acknowledged the veracity and the authority of the Old Testament prophets, he also acknowledged their limitations when he said to his own disciples:

> But blessed are your eyes, because they see; and your ears, because they hear. I tell you the truth, many prophets and righteous people longed to see what you see, but they didn't see it. And they longed to hear what you hear, but they didn't hear it (Matthew 13:16–17 NLT).

Likewise, Peter wrote,

This salvation was something even the prophets wanted to know more about when they prophesied about this gracious salvation prepared for you. They wondered what time or situation the Spirit of Christ within them was talking about when he told them in advance about Christ's suffering and his great glory afterward. They were told that their messages were not for themselves, but for you. And now this Good News has been announced to you by those who preached in the power of the Holy Spirit sent from heaven. It is all so wonderful that even the angels are eagerly watching these things happen (1 Peter 1:10–12 NLT).

All of this illustrates the idea that God does not tell everything he knows all at once. Throughout the ages, God has revealed more and more of his plan to successive generations, and Jesus is the ultimate pinnacle of God's revelation.

This helps us understand how Joel could prophesy a powerful truth more than eight hundred years before Jesus was born, and that Peter would recognize its fulfillment when the Holy Spirit was poured out on the Day of Pentecost. It is easy to understand how Joel would foresee people prophesying when the Spirit came upon them (though he also mentioned visions and dreams). He was a prophet, and when the Spirit came upon him and other prophets in his era, prophesying is what they typically did.

What Joel did not see (or at least, that he did not articulate) is that the coming of the Spirit under the new covenant would also produce numerous additional expressions of the Holy Spirit working through the lives of believers. He accurately saw that all of God's covenant people—young and old, male and female—would experience and express prophecy, visions, and dreams, but he did not necessarily envision the seven grace gifts listed in Romans 12 or the nine manifestations of the Spirit listed in 1 Corinthians 12 or the fivefold ministry offices listed in Ephesians 4. Likewise, he probably did not anticipate the vast number of *one another* scriptures articulated in the New Testament where love, comfort, encouragement, and grace would flow from one believer to another.[2]

Joel may not have known of all of the specifics that would come to the surface as the Church Age got underway, but he got us all pointed in the right direction, and for that we are thankful. He both saw and spoke of a day that was coming when the working of the Spirit would not be limited to a few select people. He foresaw God's Spirit being poured out upon all of his covenant people in such a way that holy expressions would rise from within them and flow through them.

What Joel saw is that there would be a remarkable distinction between the way ministry had taken place under the old covenant and the way it takes place now under the new covenant. Thank God that we are living in this day and age when all believers can experience the fullness of the Holy Spirit and the privilege of having God's goodness expressed through us by means of heavenly gifts and graces.

As we will discover later in this book, many kinds of expressions can come from a child of God who is under the Holy Spirit's influence, but for now, just remember that one of the reasons God puts something in you is so that he can get something out of you. I don't mean for that to sound so *transactional*, because it's really something that God intends to be *transformational*. Think in terms of what Jesus said, *"...Freely you have received, freely give"* (Matthew 10:8 NKJV). God is inviting us to discover the fullness of who he has made us to be and what he has invested in our lives. As a result, we can see the fullness of God's life displayed through all of our lives as well—both vertically (unto him) and horizontally (unto others).

THINK AND DISCUSS

1. Have you ever felt like a spectator relative to the things of God? How did you perceive yourself compared to those you felt had some kind of special status with God? What change enabled you to move beyond a spectator mentality in the church?

2. What does it mean to you to be part of *"a royal priesthood"* (1 Peter 2:9 NKJV)?

3. Paul taught that *"there is one God and one Mediator between God and men, the Man Christ Jesus"* (1 Timothy 2:5 NKJV). What implications does this have for you in your spiritual journey?

4. How has God influenced you through the indwelling and empowering of his Spirit? What kinds of expressions have resulted from his presence and activity in your life?

5. Check out Appendix D, One Another, beginning on page 205. Which of those *one another* admonitions are you doing well and regularly? Which ones could receive more attention from you?

CHAPTER TWO

WELCOME TO THE PRIESTHOOD!

Every Christian is a priest, not offering a sacrifice for sins—since that has been done once and for all—but offering his person, praise, and possessions.

—Vance Havner

What do you think of when you hear the word priest? You might think of a clergyman in a Roman Catholic, Anglican, or Orthodox church. But the concept many have of priesthood is not limited to these liturgical groups. The theme of priesthood is pervasive throughout the Old Testament, and God's priests were always associated with the offering of sacrifices. Before Aaron and his descendants became the priestly class of Israel, we meet Melchizedek, the priest and king of Salem (see Genesis 14:18) who was a type—a prophetic foreshadow—of Christist (see Psalm 110:4; Hebrews 5:10; 6:20). We also learn that the Egyptians had priests as a part of their religion.

In Exodus, we learn of Jethro (Moses' father-in-law); he was not an Israelite, but a priest of Midian (see Exodus 3:1). Later, the Bible refers to the pagan priests of Baal, Dagon, and Zeus. Priests and priestesses were abundant throughout the ancient world in a myriad of diverse religious expressions. People in certain parts of the world today would be more likely to think of Hindu or Shinto priests. Other societies still have shamans, medicine men, or even witch doctors.

The common denominator in all these—whether these people are technically called priests or not—is that they stand out from the common people of their culture or faith as a distinct class of individuals. They are perceived to have special abilities that enable them to serve as a link or mediator between the common people—the laity—and their respective deity or deities. In other words, if I am a common person, there are certain spiritual blessings I cannot receive without the help and assistance of a mediator or priest. I cannot approach God on my own or receive from him without that priest's special powers or the rituals that he might perform on my behalf.

Even though I grew up in a Protestant faith tradition that did not have priests (we used the term *pastor* when referring to the senior leader of our congregation), I still had a bit of an Old Testament priestly mentality when it came to church and spiritual things. I felt like a common person who was not extremely religious or devout, and I was entirely reliant on what I could get through the pastor and the church services to have any kind of connection with God whatsoever. I had no realization that I could have a direct, personal relationship with God through Jesus Christ. I saw myself as a spectator who lived in a distinctly separate class from those "holy men" who were preachers. I had no concept of what Paul communicated when he said, *"For there is one God and one Mediator between God and men, the Man Christ Jesus"* (1 Timothy 2:5 NKJV).

Kenneth E. Hagin articulated it so clearly:

> Under the New Covenant, all believers are made kings and priests unto God (1 Peter 2:9; Rev. 5:9,10). In other words, all believers have access to God for themselves; they don't have to go through a priest or a sacrificial system to get to God. They don't have to go through an intermediary of any kind— even a person who stands in a ministry office—in order to get to God or to receive His counsel and guidance. Of course, the

pastor has the oversight of the flock (Acts 20:28). But believers don't have to go through their pastor to get their prayers answered or to be able to communicate with God.[3]

We never want to diminish the importance of pastors or the local church; they are God's idea, and they are important. But neither do we want people failing to recognize their own sense of priesthood. Actually, the ministry of pastors and other God-called individuals is designed to cultivate and enhance the priesthood of believers, not to replace it.

Many years ago, I heard a pastor and his wife share that they hardly ever took any time off because they wanted to be available to their people 24-7. While their conscientiousness and their heart to help their people is commendable, they had come to realize that it was not good for them to never have any time off. They realized that they needed to have breaks where they could be together and simply enjoy each other's company without interruptions.

They began taking much of the day off on Mondays to simply drive, enjoy the scenery (they lived near the mountains), and build and nourish their own relationship. This was before cell phones, and they tended to feel guilty for not being accessible to their church members for those time periods. However, something happened that changed their perspective.

After one of their long Monday drives, they had two voice messages on their home phone from a church member that went something like the following:

> Voice Message # 1: "Pastor, this is _____ , and we've got a really big problem happening. We're calling to get you to pray about this. It's really important that you pray for us."
>
> Voice Message # 2 (Several hours later): "Pastor, since we didn't hear from you, we just went ahead and prayed about that situation ourselves. While we were praying, the Holy

Spirit gave us comfort and assurance about the matter, and God answered our prayer. We just wanted to let you know."

The pastor and his wife realized that they had taught their people how to pray for themselves, and that they had just witnessed the fruit of their pastoral and teaching ministry.

There is nothing wrong with reaching out to others for prayer and agreement, but we should realize that we can also pray *ourselves* and expect God to hear us. We should not think this way because we think so highly of ourselves, but because we know that we have a great High Priest named Jesus. It is through him that we have full access to the Father. When we pray to the Father in Jesus' name, we are exercising our priesthood.

How many Christians today believe that they can only receive something from God if someone else, perhaps a particularly anointed minister, prays for them? God may use certain individuals in special ways at times, but can we fully believe and wholeheartedly embrace what Jesus taught?

> *Therefore I say to **you**, whatever things **you** ask when **you** pray, believe that **you** receive them, and **you** will have them* (Mark 11:24 NKJV).

It is revolutionary for some to imagine that God would actually answer *their* prayers, but that is the assurance we have from Jesus. This is why we don't pray in our own name or based on our own merits; we exalt Jesus as our Mediator, and we approach the Father through him.

KNOW WHO YOU ARE!

We need to know who God has made us to be so that we can do what God wants us to do. Peter's declaration about the priesthood of all believers is tremendously powerful in helping us grasp the reality of our identity in Christ.

> *You also, as living stones, are being built up a spiritual house,* ***a holy priesthood****, to offer up spiritual sacrifices acceptable to God through Jesus Christ.... But you are a chosen generation,* ***a royal priesthood****, a holy nation, His own special people, that you may proclaim the praises of Him who called you out of darkness into His marvelous light* (1 Peter 2:5,9 NKJV).

When Peter referred to *a holy priesthood* and *a royal priesthood*, he was not addressing a select group of elite believers—those in some special class. No! He was writing to all Christians residing in various provinces through-out Asia Minor in what today is the nation of Turkey (see 1 Peter 1:1).

It is interesting that Peter first referred to believers as *"living stones"* and then said they *"are being built up a spiritual house"* (1 Peter 2:5). If you were to walk through a field, you might see random stones scattered all over the place. In order for a house to be built, though, someone would have to gather those stones, and then a skilled builder would have to shape the rocks, knocking off the rough edges and mortar them together according to a design.

Likewise, we as Christians are living stones, but for us to become a spiritual house, we have to have some rough edges knocked off, and then we need to be joined together. How are we held together and connected? Paul referred *"to the unity of the Spirit in the bond of peace"* (Ephesians 4:3 NKJV) and admonished that we *"be perfectly joined together in the same mind and in the same judgment"* (1 Corinthians 1:10 NKJV). Preachers sometimes refer to the building where the saints gather as the "house of God" (I've done that myself), but it's really not. We—the children of God, his holy and royal priesthood—we are the very living stones that he is building into a spiritual house. Corporately speaking, we are the house of God.

PRIVILEGES AND RESPONSIBILITIES

In writing to the seven churches of Asia Minor, John not only stated that Jesus *"loved us and washed us from our sins in His own blood,"* but also proclaimed that he *"has made us kings and priests to His God and Father"* (Revelation 1:6 NKJV). Who are we? According to the Bible, we are kings and priests unto God! Can you embrace this profound truth? Can you take ownership of it and accept this as your true identity? How few Christians realize this reality and embrace the privileges and responsibilities of the priesthood ascribed to believers in the New Testament. Followers of Jesus—all those who are born again—have both the privilege of accessing the presence and blessings of God, as well as the responsibility of sharing and conveying those blessings toward others.

The priesthood of believers is not something that is only exercised here on earth. Two vivid pictures painted in Scripture reveal to us how this same priesthood forms the identity and shapes the practice of every person in Heaven.

> *And they sang a new song with these words: "You are worthy to take the scroll and break its seals and open it. For you were slaughtered, and your blood has ransomed people for God from every tribe and language and people and nation. And you have caused them to become a Kingdom of priests for our God. And they will reign on the earth"* (Revelation 5:9–10 NLT).

Blessed and holy are those who share in the first resurrection. For them the second death holds no power, but they will be priests of God and of Christ and will reign with him a thousand years (Revelation 20:6 NLT).

Had we not read the other passages earlier, we might think this priesthood begins when we get to Heaven, but it doesn't. It begins when we are born again as children of God here on this earth. Our priesthood will continue to define us in Heaven, but it commenced the moment Jesus became our Lord, the instant we were born again.

As we begin to realize that we are kings and priests unto God, we must guard ourselves against any form of conceit or pride. This is not a status we earned or deserved. This was freely given to us, paid for by Christ's blood and graciously bestowed upon us by God. Charles Spurgeon wisely said, "Some persons on earth do not know where to put the crown; but those in heaven do. They place the diadem on the right head; and they ever sing—'And he hath made us what we are.'"[4] May the awareness of our priesthood never bring haughtiness or self-aggrandizement, but only worship and adoration.

It is vital to understand that our common priesthood does not drive us into spiritual seclusion or make others unnecessary. Rather, it is a shared status that enables us to have rich fellowship and needed interaction with one another. Paul said that we are *"individually members of one another"* (Romans 12:5 NKJV), so we should never look at our priesthood in merely individualistic terms. It is also important to recognize that even though our joint priesthood is shared equally by all believers, it does not preclude different individuals in the Body of Christ having certain gifts that equip them for certain types of ministry or for leadership roles. Priesthood makes us equally valued and loved by God, but it does not make us clones of each other in terms of our functions and abilities.

Still, our common priesthood as believers means that all believers share in certain rights, privileges, and responsibilities equally. Multiple admonitions are given to believers throughout the Book of Hebrews to take advantage of the privileges we have from and through Jesus, our Great High Priest. Here are some of the things we are beckoned to do as a community of fellow priests:

> *Let us* *therefore come boldly to the throne of grace, that we may obtain mercy and find grace to help in time of need* (Hebrews 4:16 NKJV).

> *Let us* *go on to perfection…* (Hebrews 6:1 NKJV).

> *Let us* *draw near with a true heart in full assurance of faith* (Hebrews 10:22 NKJV).

> *Let us* *hold fast the confession of our hope without wavering, for He who promised is faithful* (Hebrews 10:23 NKJV).

> *Let us* *consider one another in order to stir up love and good works* (Hebrews 10:24 NKJV).

> *Let us* *have grace, by which we may serve God acceptably with reverence and godly fear* (Hebrews 12:28 NKJV).

> *Let us* *continually offer the sacrifice of praise to God, that is, the fruit of our lips, giving thanks to His name* (Hebrews 13:15 NKJV).

Every believer can act upon these exhortations as we fulfill our priestly roles as believers. These are not assignments for some special class of Christian, and while we can and should pray for each other, someone else can't necessarily do these things on our behalf. We are, however, privileged to do these things together.

We can and should receive the grace that God makes available to each of us, and of course, we have different functions. For example, teachers can teach, evangelists can evangelize, pastors can pastor, and those with servant's hearts can serve. We share a common priesthood, but we have different expressions relative to areas of Christian service. However, no believer is called to passivity or to merely be a spectator or observer in God's wonderful family.

Those in positions of spiritual leadership are to help cultivate the priesthood of every believer, not to diminish their sense of priesthood. Leaders empower people by teaching them who they are and what they have in Christ. They also teach them to rely upon the Holy Spirit and to develop and use the gifts within them. As a Bible teacher, my job is not to make others increasingly dependent upon me, but to encourage their growing dependence on God's Word and on the Holy Spirit.

A young man I knew years ago fell into a fringe group that was very cult-like in the way they operated. He was a Bible School graduate and had participated in missionary work overseas. However, a couple of controlling, domineering leaders convinced this young man that he could never achieve his potential or fulfill his purpose unless he was under their "covering." Over time, this young man became convinced that he could not make decisions or be led by the Holy Spirit without their frequent directives. He and others in that group lived under the threat that their only real protection from Satan's power came from staying properly aligned with their leadership (i.e., living in absolute compliance to their authority, dictates, and consent).

Ultimately, he became convinced that his very spiritual survival was entirely dependent on their constant involvement and approval in every detail of his life. He literally ended up having to escape from them. By the time we met to discuss these issues, his eyes had been opened to the unhealthy control and extreme dominance these leaders were exercising in his life. In reflecting on the toxic nature of his relationship with these people, he told me, "The longer I was with them, the more I lost my sense of priesthood." While this is an extreme example, and we cringe at hearing of this type of cultic control, it is also grievous that many believers have simply never discovered the privileges and responsibilities of their priesthood.

What Does Our Priesthood Mean?

Our priesthood means that we have the privilege of direct access to God through Jesus Christ and that we are not helplessly dependent on someone else to be our mediator or link to God. Jesus, our High Priest, fulfills that role perfectly. Others can pray with and for us, just as we can pray with and for others. Priesthood does not lead us into a carnal independence from others but unites us in rich fellowship with fellow believer-priests. Together, we present ourselves to God, pray for one another, and offer up praise and worship to him.

Priesthood also conveys responsibilities; we are Christ's representatives on the earth. Paul wrote that God *"uses us to spread the knowledge of Christ everywhere, like a sweet perfume. Our lives are a Christ-like fragrance rising up to God"* (2 Corinthians 2:14–15 NLT). This is priestly language. As a matter of fact, the words *sweet aroma* are used forty-two times in the Old Testament (NKJV) to describe offerings made by the priests unto the Lord. When obedient worship took place, God smelled something that was most pleasing to him.

One of the pieces of furniture in the Tabernacle and in the Temple was called the altar of incense or the golden altar. On this altar, in the inner court, the priests would offer up incense to God. There was also an altar of brass in the outer court where animal sacrifices were made. The brass altar typified Jesus' sacrifice for sin, but the altar of incense represented worship and prayer. David prayed, *"Let my prayer be set before You as incense, the lifting up of my hands as the evening sacrifice"* (Psalm 141:2 NKJV).

There are many differences, of course, between the Old and New Testaments, but a major distinction is that today all believers are priests. Every born-again believer is a priest unto God, and it is imperative that we understand our priestly privileges and responsibilities. We should consider every aspect of our lives—our words and our actions—as expressions of worship unto God. As such, we can use our spiritual imagination to see every aspect of our lives exuding a pleasing aroma unto God.

In previous ages, only selected priests could go into the holy place, into the inner court. Only priests could offer up this incense to God. Because believers are now priests—not according to the old covenant but according to the new covenant—Paul admonished all Christians to embrace and function in their priestly duties. Let's examine several priestly activities that we are privileged to undertake.

WE FUNCTION AS PRIESTS WHEN WE OFFER OUR VERY SELVES, INCLUDING OUR BODIES, TO GOD.

There is an element of our priesthood that is intensely personal. Unlike the priests of the Old Testament, we are not offering up external things, such as grain, doves, or lambs. We are offering our very selves to God.

I urge you, brothers and sisters, in view of God's mercy, to offer your bodies as a living sacrifice, holy and pleasing to God—this is your true and proper worship (Romans 12:1 NIV).

As believer-priests, we are to offer our own bodies to God as a living and holy sacrifice! The Common English Bible renders this passage:

So, brothers and sisters, because of God's mercies, I encourage you to present your bodies as a living sacrifice that is holy and pleasing to God. This is your appropriate priestly service (Romans 12:1 CEB).

This reinforces what Paul told the Roman believers—all of them—a few chapters earlier when he admonished them to *"not present your members as instruments of unrighteousness to sin, but present yourselves to God as being alive from the dead, and your members as instruments of righteousness to God"* (Romans 6:13 NKJV). All that we have and all that we are, we are to offer unto him! This offering is a priestly duty that we have, and if we do not give God the entirety of who we are, we are robbing God of what is rightfully his.

Paul also used priestly language when writing to the Corinthians. The metaphorical imagery is slightly different, but his meaning is strong and clear:

Or didn't you realize that your body is a sacred place, the place of the Holy Spirit? Don't you see that you can't live however you please, squandering what God paid such a high price for? The physical part of you is not some piece of property belonging to the spiritual part of you. God owns the whole works. So let people see God in and through your body (1 Corinthians 6:19–20 MSG).

God purchased you so that you could be entirely his. I like to say it this way: Jesus went to the cross in the entirety of his being—spirit, soul, and body. He experienced and suffered the consequences of our sin in the entirety of his being—spirit soul, and body. He did all this so he could redeem us back to God in the entirety of our being—spirit, soul, and body. As a result, we have a priestly responsibility to present ourselves to God through our perfect High Priest, Jesus Christ.

We Function as Priests When We Worship, Praise, and Pray.

All that is expressed in our communion with God should be pleasing to him. Consider David's powerful plea:

> Let my prayer be as the evening sacrifice that burns like fragrant incense, rising as my offering to you as I lift up my hands in surrendered worship (Psalm 141:2 TPT).

A parallel idea is communicated in the New Testament. Referring to our priesthood as believers, the author of Hebrews stated, "We have an altar from which those who serve the tabernacle have no right to eat," and then admonished, "Therefore by Him let us continually offer the sacrifice of praise to God, that is, the fruit of our lips, giving thanks to His name." (Hebrews 13:10,15 NKJV). Did you catch that? The praise of our lips is a sacrifice we offer to God as his priests today.

Sometimes people assume that our time with God should primarily involve asking him for things we need, but that is not really the case. While making requests of God is a part of the equation, it is far from the whole picture. In Psalm 141, we read of "surrendered worship" and "a continual sacrifice of praise." These are no doubt pleasing to the Lord. In the Book of Acts, we see believers in Antioch spending time with God. We read, *"As they ministered to the Lord and fasted, the Holy Spirit said, 'Now separate to Me Barnabas and Saul for the work to which I have called them'"* (Acts 13:2 NKJV). Notice that they weren't asking God *for* things; they were ministering *to* him.

The word *ministered* in Acts 13:2 is sometimes translated *worship* in other English translations, and in the Septuagint (Greek) version of the Old Testament, this same word is often used to describe the functions of Hebrew priests as they ministered in both the Tabernacle and the Temple. In other words, worship (or ministering to the Lord) is a priestly function in which New Testament believers can fully participate. We even see this from Heaven's perspective in the Book of Revelation. John wrote:

> *And when he took the scroll, the four living beings and the twenty-four elders fell down before the Lamb. Each one had a harp, and they held gold bowls filled with incense, which are the prayers of God's people* (Revelation 5:8 NLT).

> *Then another angel with a gold incense burner came and stood at the altar. And a great amount of incense was given to him to mix with the prayers of God's people as an offering on the gold altar before the throne. The smoke of the incense, mixed with the prayers of God's holy people, ascended up to God from the altar where the angel had poured them out* (Revelation 8:3–4 NLT).

Even as I write this, I am seriously challenged to consider what happens when I pray, when I praise, and when I worship. Am I mindful that at such times I am ministering as a priest before the Lord?

Jonathan Edwards, a great pastor during America's First Great Awakening said the following regarding the praise of believers:

This spiritual priesthood offers to God the sacrifice of praise. Many of their sacrifices under the law were sacrifices of peace offerings, which were mostly for thanksgiving and praise. But the spiritual sacrifice of the hearty and sincere praises of a saint, are more acceptable to God than all the bulls, and rams, and he-goats that they offered. The heartfelt praises of one true Christian are of more account with God than all those two and twenty thousand oxen, and a hundred and twenty thousand sheep, which Solomon offered to God at the dedication of the temple.[5]

What an amazing statement. We don't have to look back longingly to the "good old days" when priests offered animal sacrifices. We live in the better new days when we offer our praise and our hearts to the living God!

As priests, we have genuine access to God—to his ear and to his heart. Paul wrote, *"Now all of us can come to the Father through the same Holy Spirit because of what Christ has done for us"* (Ephesians 2:18 NLT). We should never take lightly the great privilege we have of approaching and communicating with him. David saw his prayer rising as a fragrant incense to God and understood it was an offering unto him. As priests, we are not to simply go through religious motions in a ritualistic manner. Instead, we are to minister unto the Lord with our whole heart.

WE FUNCTION AS PRIESTS WHEN WE SERVE.

One of the most moving stories in Scripture is found in John's Gospel.

Six days before the Passover celebration began, Jesus arrived in Bethany, the home of Lazarus—the man he had raised from the dead. A dinner was prepared in Jesus' honor. Martha served, and Lazarus was among those who ate with him. Then Mary took a twelve-ounce jar of expensive perfume made from essence of nard, and she anointed Jesus' feet with it, wiping his feet with her hair. The house was filled with the fragrance (John 12:1–3 NLT).

In this story, Mary was not technically a priest, but she operated as a servant motivated by profound love and devotion. However, there is a similarity to what happened when the priests served at the altar of incense in that *"the house was filled with the fragrance."* If the house was filled with the fragrance of that perfume, can you imagine what Mary's garment and hair were like? She would have borne the same fragrance.

Have you ever been in a smoke-filled room for any length of time? After you left, you reeked of smoke. Likewise, when Old Testament priests ministered in the holy place at the altar of incense, the beautiful fragrance would become infused in their robes and even their hair. When they later walked among the people, it would be obvious that they had been in a holy place, in the very presence of God. The same should be true of us. When we serve as unto the Lord, we should be like Mary. We are not to engage in acts of service grudgingly or with a complaining heart; rather, our labors are to be labors of love, expressing heartfelt devotion to the Lord.

Our service to others should also be from the heart, as an act of worship unto God. Remember what Jesus said, *"When you did it to one of the least of these my brothers and sisters, you were doing it to me!"* (Matthew 25:40 NLT). When we serve others as unto the Lord, an aroma of Christ is released. When we emulate the servant's heart that Mary demonstrated, it affects the spiritual atmosphere all around us. All that we are, all that we say, and all that we do should reflect the love and nature of who God is. We are his hands and his feet in the earth. As his ambassadors, we serve one another, and our lives bear testimony of God's love to the world.

In the last section ("We Function as Priests When We Worship, Praise, and Pray."), I referenced Hebrews 13:15, which speaks of the praise of our lips being a sacrifice we offer to God. The very next verse contains priestly language as well. *"And don't forget to do good and to share with those in need. These are the sacrifices that please God"* (Hebrews 13:16 NLT). I especially like the way the Message renders this passage:

> *Make sure you don't take things for granted and go slack in working for the common good; share what you have with others. God takes particular pleasure in acts of worship—a different kind of "sacrifice"—that take place in kitchen and workplace and on the streets* (Hebrews 13:16 MSG).

Doing good and serving others can absolutely be a priestly work when we do it from the heart to glorify God. The final part of that—sharing with others—brings us to our next point.

WE FUNCTION AS PRIESTS WHEN WE GIVE.

One of the functions of priests in the Old Testament was to receive offerings from the hands of the common people and present them to God. The priests in those days were the go-betweens, standing between God and people. However, in the New Testament, there are no common people among believers. Recognizing our immortal nature, C. S. Lewis remarked, "There are no *ordinary* people. You have never talked to a mere mortal."[6] We are all priests (or in the case of unbelievers, potential priests), and therefore, we have the privilege of presenting our gifts directly to God through our Great High Priest, Jesus.

Whether a particular gift is given to our local church or to another type of ministry, the attitude of our hearts should reflect Paul's description of the generosity of his friends in Philippi.

> I've received the gift you sent by Epaphroditus and viewed it as a sweet sacrifice, perfumed with the fragrance of your faithfulness, which is so pleasing to God (Philippians 4:18 TPT).

Because this verse is often read when offerings are received in churches, believers may get the impression that all giving is looked upon by God in such favorable and glowing terms, but that is not the case. A quick review of the story of Ananias and Saphira (see Acts 5:1–11) will confirm how much motives and attitudes matter when it comes to giving.

The first chapter of Malachi also reveals that not all giving is pleasing to God. Those the prophet addressed were not honoring God with their best, nor were they showing respect to God in their giving (see Malachi 1:6–8). In short, they did not fear God, and their hearts were not inclined toward obedience. In contrast to the errant giving by his covenant people, God envisioned a day when those in other nations would give in a way that pleased him.

> My name will be great among the nations, from where the sun rises to where it sets. In every place incense and pure offerings will be brought to me, because my name will be great among the nations," says the Lord Almighty (Malachi 1:11 NIV).

The Philippians were people from one of those other nations, and their generous hearts match the description given by Malachi. As we just read, Paul described their giving as "a sweet sacrifice, perfumed with the fragrance of your faithfulness" (Philippians 4:18 TPT).

In order for our giving to be as a sweet incense unto the Lord, it must be done in faith and obedience, and most of all, it must be motivated by love. Paul wrote, *"And though I bestow all my goods to feed the poor, and though I give my body to be burned, but have not love, it profits me nothing"* (1 Corinthians 13:3 NKJV). When we are motivated by love, our giving is seen as worship unto the Lord; it is pleasing to him, and we most certainly profit.

Whatever we give to God materially should simply be an extension of a life and heart that has been totally given to him. When Paul described the extravagant generosity of the Macedonian believers, he remarked, *"They even did more than we had hoped, for their first action was to give themselves to the Lord and to us, just as God wanted them to do"* (2 Corinthians 8:5 NLT). Their giving was not just a token, but it reflected lives that had been totally dedicated and consecrated to God. Thus, their generosity was of a priestly nature.

WE FUNCTION AS PRIESTS WHEN WE EVANGELIZE.

When we share the gospel with others, we are communicating a message that provides them with access to God. We are certainly not their mediator; only Jesus can fulfill that role. But we can be the messengers of the gospel, and it is the gospel that enables people to come to God through Jesus. Paul used priestly terminology when he described the evangelistic process.

> *Yet I have written you quite boldly on some points to remind you of them again, because of the grace God gave me to be a minister of Christ Jesus to the Gentiles. He gave me the priestly duty of proclaiming the gospel of God, so that the Gentiles might become an offering acceptable to God, sanctified by the Holy Spirit* (Romans 15:15–16 NIV).

This powerful passage reveals that our priestly responsibilities are not just about *worshipping* God, but also include our *witness* to the world. How does this process work? What does it mean to function as a priest relative to winning the lost? Paul elaborated on this in his second epistle to the Corinthians. The apostle wrote that God has not only *"brought us back to himself through Christ,"* but also *"has given us this task of reconciling people to him"* (2 Corinthians 5:18 NLT). Paul then gave even more amplification and told us that God *"gave us this wonderful message of reconciliation,"* and that as *"Christ's ambassadors; God is making his appeal through us. We speak for Christ when we plead, 'Come back to God!'"* (2 Corinthians 5:19–20 NLT). Our priestly function is fulfilled when we share what Paul called, *"this wonderful message of reconciliation."*

It is vital to understand the difference between being a *representative* as opposed to a *mediator*. As priests, we represent God when we share the message. However, we are not pointing people to ourselves, but rather to Jesus. Earlier in 2 Corinthians, Paul explained, *"You see, we don't go around preaching about ourselves. We preach that Jesus Christ is Lord, and we ourselves are your servants for Jesus' sake"* (2 Corinthians 4:5 NLT). As his representatives, we point to the mediator, the Lord Jesus Christ. He is the High Priest and the only true mediator between God and people.

Some might object, thinking only "official preachers" have what Paul called *"the priestly duty of proclaiming the gospel of God"* (Romans 15:16 NIV). It is true that some people have an official assignment and anointing to preach the gospel (more on that later), but every Christian can be a witness and share the gospel, even though they may never stand behind a pulpit in a sanctuary or auditorium.

Consider what happened in the first century when a great persecution arose against the church following the death of Stephen. As a result, many believers fled Jerusalem for their safety. Acts 8:4 reads, *"Therefore those who were scattered went everywhere preaching the word"* (NKJV). People have often read that and thought, "Of course, the apostles all preached as they traveled." However, that is not at all what that text is telling us. As a matter of fact, a previous verse states, *"...At that time a great persecution arose against the church which was at Jerusalem; and they were all scattered throughout the regions of Judea and Samaria, **except the apostles***" (Acts 8:1 NKJV).

When we see these two verses together, we understand that it was all of the other believers—not the apostles—who were scattered abroad and shared the gospel. In a broad sense, this *"priestly duty of proclaiming the gospel of God"* belongs to every Christian, not just to those who are called to what we describe as the fivefold ministry (see Ephesians 4:11). When people respond to the gospel, they not only pass from darkness into light, but God also receives them as a living sacrifice, an offering that is well pleasing to him. What a privilege it is for us to "offer them to God" in this glorious way.

The priesthood of the believer is not simply a catchy religious phrase, but it summarizes expressions that are a dynamic part of our relationship with God. These expressions should flow freely from a heart that has been transformed by his wonderful grace!

- We Function as Priests When We Offer Our Very Selves, Including Our Bodies, to God.

- We Function as Priests When We Worship, Praise, and Pray.

- We Function as Priests When We Serve.

- We Function as Priests When We Give.

- We Function as Priests When We Evangelize.

Why do we do these things? Because we are priests unto our God, and these are things that priests do.

But there is more to the priesthood than just engaging in the above-mentioned activities. We can walk out our priesthood through everything we do. I mentioned Romans 12:1 earlier in this chapter, but the Message version really brings it home: *"Take your everyday, ordinary life—your sleeping, eating, going-to-work, and walking-around life—and place it before God as an offering."* This same comprehensive approach to a priestly, God-conscious life is also prescribed in Paul's statement, *"And whatever you do in word or deed, do all in the name of the Lord Jesus, giving thanks to God the Father through Him"* (Colossians 3:17 NKJV).

REFLECT AND DISCUSS

1. What does Vance Havner's quote at the very beginning of the chapter mean to you? He said, "Every Christian is a priest, not offering a sacrifice for sins—since that has been done once and for all—but offering his person, praise, and possessions." Do you have that sense of priesthood in your relationship with God?

2. Peter wrote that we are *"living stones… being built up a spiritual house"* (1 Peter 2:5 NKJV). How well connected are you with others who are also living stones? Have you ever had to have any rough edges knocked off in order to be better connected with others?

3. Review the "Let Us" list on page 34. Have you been aware of actively fulfilling these admonitions throughout your spiritual journey? Have you been mindful of engaging in these practices in recent times?

4. In this chapter, we learned that our priesthood carries with it both privilege and responsibility. Do you think believers are more inclined to think of their priestly privileges or their priestly responsibilities? What is the basis for your answer?

5. How inclined are you to think of your priesthood when you:

- Offer yourself and your body to God?
- Worship, praise, and pray?
- Serve?
- Give?
- Evangelize?

CHAPTER THREE

PETER SPEAKS: EACH ONE HAS RECEIVED

It is a rare church whose members all put their shoulder to the wheel. The typical church is composed of the few whose shoulders are bruised by their faithful labors and the many who are unwilling to raise a blister in the service of God and their fellowmen.

—A. W. Tozer[7]

In the last chapter, we referenced Peter telling all believers that they comprise a holy and a royal priesthood (see 1 Peter 2:5,9). In the very first chapter, we saw the apostle Peter quoting Joel's prophecy—God's Spirit has been poured out on all flesh, and the sons and daughters, as well as menservants and maidservants, will prophesy. In addition, both young and old men will have things supernaturally revealed to them (see Acts 2:16–18). No longer will just the prophet, priest, and king have the anointing of the Holy Spirit, as it had been throughout the Old Testament. Now, all believers will have God's Spirit dwelling within them and can be empowered by God's Spirit to work for him.

Though he quoted Joel's prophecy on the Day of Pentecost, Peter's understanding and appreciation for the fullness of God's plan grew over the years; he gained further insight beyond what Joel originally understood or expressed. Having been an Old Testament prophet, Joel was primarily familiar with prophecy as an expression of the Holy Spirit's work, but Peter came to see that in the New Testament—in the age of the church—there was a much greater diversity beyond prophesying when it came to the operations of the Holy Spirit. Having matured and grown in understanding, Peter later admonished believers:

> As each one has received a gift, minister it to one another, as good stewards of the manifold grace of God. If anyone speaks, let him speak as the oracles of God. If anyone ministers, let him do it as with the ability which God supplies, that in all things God may be glorified through Jesus Christ, to whom belong the glory and the dominion forever and ever. Amen (1 Peter 4:10–11 NKJV).

These two verses are absolutely loaded with rich meaning when it comes to understanding that every believer is called to do something for God.

Nothing Peter said in the above verse contradicts Joel's prophecy, the one he quoted many years earlier, but he certainly amplified what Joel originally said. Whereas Joel used the *"all flesh"* terminology, Peter flatly stated, *"God has given each of you a gift from his great variety of spiritual gifts"* (1 Peter 4:10 NLT). In concept, they both refer to everybody.

Because of his perspective at the time, Joel spoke primarily of prophesying, but Peter pointed out that God has made a great assortment of gifts and tools available for all of his people during this new era. Peter referred to God's *"great variety of spiritual gifts."* The Passion Translation renders that same verse—1 Peter 4:10—as *"Every believer has received grace gifts, so use them to serve one another as faithful stewards of the many-colored tapestry of God's grace."*

Peter proceeded to delineate between two major categories of these God-given gifts by means of the following questions. First, he asked, *"Do you have the gift of speaking?"* and then he inquired, *"Do you have the gift of helping others?"* Let's explore both of these.

THE GIFT OF SPEAKING

It seems that Peter was using very broad terms when he asked about people having the gift of speaking. The reason I say this is because the New Testament describes a wide variety of speaking-type ministries. These would include such things as preaching, teaching, admonishing, exhorting, prophesying, and so forth. While any Christian can speak a word of kindness to another or share an encouraging thought, some have specific gifts when it comes to communicating verbally.

Peter's full statement is, *"Do you have the gift of speaking? Then speak as though God himself were speaking through you"* (1 Peter 4:11 NLT). What Peter was describing is different than a person simply having natural skill in communicating. Though there could be an overlap, and natural skills and training can be good, Peter was describing a divinely imparted, supernaturally based gift. Here is a bit of what I've observed about this type of gift over the years.

In my own experience, I did not have an inclination toward public speaking during my younger years. In high school, I took a course or two that involved public speaking, but it was not something that I especially enjoyed or aspired to. As a matter of fact, as the president of my senior class, I was invited to speak at my high school graduation ceremony. I actually declined this opportunity, as I simply had no desire to stand before a large crowd and give an address.

Around three weeks after I graduated from high school, I had an encounter with the Lord and was filled with the Holy Spirit. It was a real turning point in my life, and I quickly developed a love and hunger for the Word of God. For the first time in my life, Scripture became very real and meaningful to me. I sensed the life in God's Word, and as it ministered to me, I wanted to share those same truths with others. Unlike the time before I was filled with the Spirit, I now had something I wanted to say!

I did not start out preaching substantive or full-length sermons, but I enjoyed sharing a Scripture or two at fellowship meetings. A gift was beginning to surface even though I had much growing yet to do. This soon evolved into sharing complete lessons and longer series of messages. More than four decades later, I continue to find great joy in speaking to groups of all sizes, whether it is to a gathering of a handful of people or to thousands. I recognize that there is always a sense of divine enablement when I stand before people and share God's Word.

Gifts involving preaching and teaching can be cultivated and developed through training, practice, and experience. As a teacher in a Bible School for many years, I had the privilege of facilitating many preaching labs in which young Bible School students would have twelve minutes to deliver a message they had written. It was a joy seeing the gift percolating within them and being expressed as they spoke, even if that gift was in embryonic form at the time. It was an even greater joy to hear them preach years later as their God-given abilities and effectiveness had greatly increased and expanded.

The Gift of Helping Others

Apparently, not everyone is called to a speaking (or pulpit) type of ministry. After referring to those who minister by the spoken word, Peter then stated, *"...Do you have the gift of helping others? Do it with all the strength and energy that God supplies..."* (1 Peter 4:11 NLT).

In churches all over the world I have observed tremendous contributions made by those who do not necessarily stand behind the pulpit, but who serve faithfully behind the scenes. Such unsung heroes may not be highly visible in what they do, but churches cannot survive or thrive without great helpers.

BEYOND THE TWO CATEGORIES

Beyond Peter telling us that we have all received grace—some to speak and some to serve—he also gave numerous illustrations about how believers are to be engaged in expressing the life of Christ. The descriptions below from Peter's first epistle all reinforce the idea that the Christian faith is not one of passive spectatorship, but profound involvement from the core of our being. The life of God is to be expressed in the transformation of our character, actions, and relationships.

Christians are called to:

- A Rejoicing Life—"...*You rejoice with joy inexpressible and full of glory*" (1 Peter 1:8 NKJV).

- A Vigilant Life—"*So prepare your minds for action and exercise self-control...*" (1 Peter 1:13 NLT).

- A Holy Life—"*You must be holy in everything you do, just as God who chose you is holy*" (1 Peter 1:15 NLT).

- A Trusting Life—"*Through Christ you have come to trust in God. And you have placed your faith and hope in God...*" (1 Peter 1:21 NLT).

- A Loving Life—"...*You must show sincere love to each other as brothers and sisters.... Continue to show deep love for each other...*" (1 Peter 1:22; 4:8 NLT).

- A Transformed Life—"*Get rid of all evil behavior. Be done with all deceit, hypocrisy, jealousy, and all unkind speech*" (1 Peter 2:1 NLT).

- A Priestly Life—"...*Through the mediation of Jesus Christ, you offer spiritual sacrifices that please God*" (1 Peter 2:5 NLT).

- A Proclaiming Life—"...*That you may proclaim the praises of Him who called you out of darkness into His marvelous light*" (1 Peter 2:9 NKJV).

- A Virtuous Life—"*This is the will of God, that by doing good you may put to silence the ignorance of foolish men*" (1 Peter 2:15 NKJV).

- An Honoring Life—"*Honor all people. Love the brotherhood. Fear God. Honor the king*" (1 Peter 2:17 NKJV).

- A Unified, Compassionate, and Humble Life—"*Be like-minded, be sympathetic, love one another, be compassionate and humble*" (1 Peter 3:8 NIV).

- A Prepared Life—"...*Always be prepared to give an answer to everyone who asks you to give the reason for the hope that you have...*" (1 Peter 3:15 NIV).

- A Prayerful Life—"...*Be serious and watchful in your prayers*" (1 Peter 4:7 NKJV).

- A Hospitable Life—"*Be hospitable to one another...*" (1 Peter 4:9 NKJV).

- A Stalwart Life—"*Stay alert! Watch out for your great enemy, the devil. He prowls around like a roaring lion, looking for someone to devour. Stand firm against him, and be strong in your faith...*" (1 Peter 5:8–9 NLT).

As you read that very powerful list of the lives we are called to live, I hope you kept in mind that every single one of these descriptions is from a single, relatively brief New Testament epistle, 1 Peter.

If you are one who preaches and teaches, or if you are one who actively engages in acts of service in your church and relationships, you are fulfilling God's plan. All of these are important, and God's people are graced for such endeavors. However, beyond these kinds of work, we are also called to actively express the nature and the character of God through our lifestyles. We are not mere spectators to matters regarding faith; we are called to a Christian life of full engagement.

IF I'M A PRIEST, DO I NEED OTHER BELIEVERS? DO I NEED A PASTOR?

Our priesthood as believers should not separate us or drive us into isolation from one another. Rather, our mutual priesthood should strengthen our bonds and lead us into stronger fellowship and partnership with one another. The fact that each of us has received something of value from the Spirit of God should create greater avenues of sharing and interaction among us. Do you remember Peter's statement that we examined earlier in this chapter? It begins, "*As each one has received a gift, minister it to one another...*" (1 Peter 4:10 NKJV). We can never forget the *one another* aspect of who we are in Christ.

Unfortunately, not all have processed or applied their sense of priesthood correctly. Henry and Tom Blackaby noted:

It is so evident that many leaders have never known, or have simply forgotten, the corporate and interdependent nature of God's call on their lives. Each sees himself more as a "royal priest" than as part of a "royal priesthood."[8]

In the natural, if we are citizens of a particular country, we have all the rights and privileges of citizenship in that specific nation. I am a citizen of the United States, and I have equal rights and privileges (as well as responsibilities) with every other citizen. I am not superior or inferior to anyone. That doesn't mean, though, that I don't need the help of other people or that I can't help them.

Many times in my life, I have needed the help of and have benefitted from the skills and abilities of numerous others, such as plumbers, dentists, electricians, mechanics, doctors, and accountants, just to name a few. The fact that they have skills that I don't have doesn't mean they are more of a citizen than I am. It simply means, as a citizen, I don't have every skill that could possibly be possessed.

Even though all of God's children have all of the rights and privileges of being the sons and daughters of God—of priesthood—we don't all have the same gifts, maturity, or background experiences. The fact that I am a priest unto God (having full access to him as well as responsibilities from him), does not make other believers unnecessary in my life. I can still benefit greatly from those who have gifts that I may lack.

Having or lacking certain gifts and skills does not make us superior or inferior to anyone. Being born of the Spirit, we all have the same basic rights as the sons and daughters of God even though different ones are gifted for particular tasks. We can all have a rich relationship with God even though we have different abilities and can make different types of contributions to our fellow believers. The fact that I am a priest unto God does not mean I should take the microphone and try to sing in front of the congregation. I am not called or gifted to do that. Likewise, a person should not say, "We are all priests in the Body of Christ, so I have just as much of a right to preach (or to run the church) as anyone else." No! If we're not called and gifted that way, we should not try to engage in those ministries.

It might help us to think of the fact that we are all equal in one sense, and yet we are all different in another sense. Let's say that a mom and dad have three children. All three children are one hundred per cent equal in that they are each a child of their parents; they are each equally loved and valued as members of the family. One may be musically gifted, another may be academically talented, and the third may excel in athletics. Each of these children is completely a member of that family and has all the rights and privileges of being a member of that family, but they have different areas of ability and can each perform more effectively in different settings.

It would be most unfortunate if people were to discover their priest-hood in Christ and then decide that they don't need a pastor or do not need to be a part of a local church. Your priesthood does not take the place of having a pastor or relating in a healthy manner to other believers. Rather, your priesthood enhances your membership in the Body of Christ. There is a sense in which we are all equal, but there is a sense in which we are all equipped to minister in different ways and in different capacities. In the next chapter, we will explore how Paul amplified the same principles Peter shared and how he communicated about the amazing diversity of gifts springing from the grace of God in the lives of believers.

THINK AND DISCUSS

1. Consider Peter's statement in 1 Peter 4:10. What does each of these statements mean to you?

   - *As each one has received a gift…*
   - *minister it to one another…*
   - *as good stewards of the manifold grace of God.*

2. Peter delineated those who are gifted to speak and those who are gifted to serve. Which of these do you think best describes you? Name some people you know who fit in each of these categories.

3. Review the bulleted list beginning on page 55. In considering the kind of life a Christian is called to live, rate your progress in each of the areas. In which areas do you believe you are strong, and in which areas do you believe you can benefit from growth?

4. How would you respond to this question: "If we are all priests, then why would we need each other? Why would we need to have the influence of a pastor and other leaders in our lives?"

CHAPTER FOUR

PAUL AMPLIFIES: GIFTS DIFFERING

Paul clearly teaches that each Christian believer ought to demonstrate a proper gift or gifts, bestowed by God the Holy Spirit, and that together the believers should accomplish the work of God as a team.

—A. W. Tozer[9]

Peter's simple breakdown in 1 Peter 4:11 demonstrates that some in the Body of Christ have gifts that enable them to minister by speaking, while others minister through serving and helping others. While Peter spoke broadly, within those two categories are many sub-categories. We will learn in this chapter how Paul captured and expanded these.

In other words, there are various types of both speaking and serving. All speaking and all serving does not look the same. However, every single member of the Body of Christ has received some type of grace-based gift from God with an accompanying responsibility to use it.

For as we have many members in one body, but all the members do not have the same function, so we, being many, are one body in Christ, and individually members of one another. Having then gifts differing according to the grace that is given to us, let us use them: if prophecy, let us prophesy in proportion to our faith; or ministry, let us use it in our ministering; he who teaches, in teaching; he who exhorts, in exhortation; he who gives, with liberality; he who leads, with diligence; he who shows mercy, with cheerfulness (Romans 12:4–8 NKJV).

Notice what Paul did *not* write in verse four. He did *not* state, "not all the members have a function." Rather, he asserted that *"all the members do not have **the same** function."*

It is vital that we understand this distinction. If Paul had taught that not all members in the Body of Christ have a function, then pastors would need to get up and tell their congregations that many believers have no use, function, or purpose. There would be, by divine design, two radically divergent groups in the Body of Christ—those with and those without a function. The implication of Paul's statement is that all believers *have* a function; they just don't all have the *same* function.

And then, so that we don't get caught up focusing exclusively on our own giftedness, Paul immediately stressed the collective nature of our identity: *"We... are one body in Christ, and individually members of one another"* (Romans 12:5 NKJV). This reminder—that we are members of one another—helps prevent us from having an isolated perspective of ourselves. I really can't exercise my gift properly unless I am vitally connected to others.

Some people errantly believe they can have "church" all by themselves. You might have heard someone say, "Well, I don't really go to church any-where. I just have a personal relationship with God." Such an individual might tell you that they never worship with other believers, but instead, just take their Bible to the coffee shop and read it—that doing that is their form of having church. Really, though, that is not church; that is having devotions. It's great that a person reads their Bible on their own—we encourage that. But if we really read our Bibles, eventually we're going to come across the passage that says, *"Let us not neglect our meeting together, as some people do, but encourage one another, especially now that the day of his return is drawing near"* (Hebrews 10:25 NLT).

We are individuals and there is a legitimate sense in which we have a personal relationship with God, but we can't really be a blessing and help to others if we have a hyper-individualistic mindset. Norman Vincent Peale expressed this same thought:

> The man who lives for himself is a failure. Even if he gains much wealth, position or fortune, he is still a failure. The man who lives for others has achieved true success. A rich man who consecrates his wealth and his position to the good of humanity is a success.

While divinely imparted abilities are ours to steward, they really exist for the benefit of others. John Wesley recognized our need for connectedness and noted that he had been advised as a young man that "You must therefore find companions or make them. The Bible knows nothing of solitary religion."

I can do certain things with my gifts individually, and you can do certain things with your gifts individually. However, when several of us combine our gifts and work together toward a common goal and purpose, the effectiveness of our combined gifts skyrockets exponentially. Billy Graham recognized this concept when he stated:

> I realize more than ever that this ministry has been a team effort. Without the help of our prayer partners, our financial supporters, our staff, and our board of directors—this ministry and all of our dreams to spread the Good News of God's love throughout the world would not have been possible.[10]

Graham and his team operated on a worldwide scale, but every team can achieve far more when the contributing members recognize that they are *"individually members of one another."*

The New Living Translation renders the first part of Romans 12:6 as, *"In his grace, God has given us different gifts for doing certain things well...."* Peter had alluded to different categories of gifts—speaking and serving—when he referred to God's *"great variety of spiritual gifts"* (1 Peter 4:10 NLT). This correlates to Paul communicating that we don't all have the same function, and then Paul proceeded to get significantly more detailed than Peter did.

THOSE WHO SPEAK

Paul mentioned three specific types of speaking: prophecy, teaching, and exhortation. Let's look at each of these.

Prophecy

> *...if God has given you the ability to prophesy, speak out with as much faith as God has given you* (Romans 12:6 NLT).

Unfortunately, when many people hear prophecy mentioned, they simply think of foretelling the future. While that element may appear at certain times, the New Testament emphasis is somewhat different. Paul explained that *"one who prophesies strengthens others, encourages them, and comforts them"* (1 Corinthians 14:3 NLT). In the context of a gathering of believers, he also stated that *"...one who speaks a word of prophecy strengthens the entire church"* (1 Corinthians 14:4 NLT).

When Peter quoted Joel on the Day of Pentecost, he made it very clear that the outpouring of the Holy Spirit would result in many of God's children speaking by divine inspiration.

> *This is what I will do in the last days—I will pour out my Spirit on everybody and cause your sons and daughters to prophesy....*

The Holy Spirit will come upon all my servants, men and women alike, and they will prophesy (Acts 2:17–18 TPT).

These statements do not mean that all believers become prophets in the fivefold sense of the term (see Ephesians 4:11), but simply that the Holy Spirit can and does inspire believers to speak words that strengthen and encourage others. The Holy Spirit will help us fulfill what Solomon described when he said, *"...A word spoken in due season, how good it is!"* (Proverbs 15:23 NKJV).

This does not mean our statements need to be religious-sounding or peppered with phrases such as "Thus saith the Lord." You can speak relationally with others, in your normal tone of voice, and simply be inspired by the Holy Spirit to speak kind, encouraging, and uplifting words that bring the fresh air of God's presence into another person's life or perhaps to a group. Prophesying does not imply that you are trying to predict the future or discern mysterious secrets in their lives; you are simply sharing God-anointed, Spirit-breathed words with them.

Teaching

...If you are a teacher, teach well (Romans 12:7 NLT).

Just as some are given grace by the Holy Spirit to speak inspirationally to bring edification, others are given grace to speak instructionally to bring understanding. Teaching has been a vital means of communicating God's truth for untold centuries. For example, when the people of God returned from Babylonian captivity, teaching re-emerged in a notable and powerful way.

Ezra the scribe stood on a high wooden platform that had been made for the occasion.... Ezra stood on the platform in full view of all the people. When they saw him open the book, they all rose to their feet. Then Ezra praised the LORD, the great God, and all the people chanted, "Amen! Amen!" as they lifted their hands. Then they bowed down and worshiped the LORD with their faces to the ground. The Levites...then instructed the people in the Law while everyone remained in their places. **They read from the Book of the Law of God and clearly explained the meaning of what was being read, helping the people understand each passage** (Nehemiah 8:4–8 NLT).

Notice the components of teaching here:

- They read Scripture verbatim—word for word.
- They clearly explained the meaning of what they had just read.
- They helped the people understand each passage.

When minds are open and hearts are eager to learn, teaching is one of the most powerful tools, gifts, or functions that God has placed in his church.

Consider how Jesus and Paul operated in the area of teaching. Luke recorded that when the Lord walked with two disciples on the road to Emmaus after his resurrection, *"Jesus took them through the writings of Moses and all the prophets, explaining from all the Scriptures the things concerning himself"* (Luke 24:27 NLT). Later, those two disciples *"said to each other, 'Didn't our hearts burn within us as he talked with us on the road and explained the Scriptures to us?'"* (Luke 24:32 NLT). Teaching should be life-giving; it absolutely does not need to be—nor should it be—dry and boring!

When Paul met with Jews in Rome, Luke wrote that Paul:

explained and testified about the Kingdom of God and tried to persuade them about Jesus from the Scriptures. Using the law of Moses and the books of the prophets, he spoke to them from morning until evening (Acts 28:23 NLT).

Teaching sessions don't have to be long and protracted to be effective, but in another case, Paul met with a group of believers to celebrate communion and ended up speaking until midnight. He was "interrupted" long enough to raise a young man from the dead who had fallen out of a third-floor window. He then resumed teaching until dawn (see Acts 20:7–12).

Teaching doesn't always have to be done by professional clergy, nor is everyone who has been graced to teach been called to teach the Body of Christ at large. Thank God for countless Sunday School teachers and home group leaders who help others grow by teaching important truths from God's Word. Also, many who do an excellent job teaching in one-on-one situations would not feel comfortable with a large crowd. A person doesn't have to have a public platform to convey vital information to others.

Consider Priscilla and Aquila who heard Apollos preach in Ephesus. They recognized the limitations of his knowledge, and in parental fashion, they *"...took him aside and explained the way of God even more accurately"* (Acts 18:26 NLT). Teaching can be brief or extended, simple or in-depth, private or public, one-on-one or to great crowds, informal or formal.

Think of the term *driver*. Someone might drive a bus full of students, or even a semi-truck that hauls massive amounts of products across the country. Someone else might be a race car driver with NASCAR, while another is a hospitality worker behind the wheel of a golf-cart that picks up people in a hospital parking lot and delivers them to the front entrance. All of these people might be called *drivers,* but the type of work they do and their respective capacities and abilities vary drastically. The same concept applies to various teachers relative to their diverse roles and functions.

Exhortation[11]

> *If your gift is to encourage others, be encouraging...* (Romans
> 12:8 NLT).

A Bible Dictionary states that the word *exhortation* is a:

> Translation of a Greek word literally meaning "a calling of
> someone alongside to help." Its primary meaning in the NT is
> the urging of someone to do something—particularly some
> ethical course of action. In some contexts, the same Greek
> word may also include the idea of comforting and consoling.
> The given context will determine which meaning to use.[12]

Whereas teaching is more logical and instructional, exhortation seems
to be more of an appeal—something more motivational in nature. Beyond
informing (teaching), exhorting is often an urging for another person to
do something, an encouragement to move forward. Exhorters are often
considered to be strong motivators who light a fire under people and stir
people to action.

Because these different verbal gifts often have similarities, we sometimes see an overlap when Paul mentions them. It might be helpful to
think of prophecy, teaching, and exhortation as three petals on the same
flower. These expressions are complementary and can work well together;
they are not contradictory. For example, Paul told the Corinthians that
*"he who prophesies speaks edification and **exhortation** and comfort to men"*
(1 Corinthians 14:3 NKJV). Similarly, he told Timothy, *"Till I come, give
attention to reading, to **exhortation**, to doctrine"* (1 Timothy 4:13 NKJV).

In another place, Paul told Timothy to *"teach and **exhort** these things"* (1
Timothy 6:2 NKJV). Apparently, these are not identical, or Paul would have
been repeating himself. We also see the value and necessity of this type of

expression as the author of Hebrews advised believers to *"**exhort** one another daily"* (Hebrews 3:13 NKJV). The Amplified Bible renders this passage, *"But instead warn (admonish, urge, and encourage) one another every day."*

It is important to note that this was not written only to pastors or other preachers, but to believers in general. Believers were told to exhort one another. As God graces us, we can and should exhort (admonish, urge, encourage, motivate, appeal to, and light a fire under) each other regularly! How many believers could respond to the grace of God and engage more often in this vital expression of God's love?

THOSE WHO SERVE

Paul also referred to four expressions of grace that can manifest away from the pulpit: ministry (or serving), giving, leading, and mercy. Let's look at each of these individually.

Ministry

> *If your gift is serving others, serve them well...* (Romans 12:7 NLT).

Some translations refer to this as *ministering* and others describe it as *serving*. Over many years, the words *minister* or *ministry* seem to have taken on a connotation of professional clergy in the minds of most people, but biblically it is used far more broadly than that. I have known of many cases where someone would come up to a person who was actively helping in a local church, and ask them, "When are you going to go into the ministry?" Perhaps that individual does not have a certain title or preach from behind a pulpit, but technically, if that person is serving God then he or she is already in the ministry.

The word *diakonia* is one of the Greek words for servant (it is where we get our English word *deacon*) and broadly refers to serving. This divinely graced function of serving is likely very similar if not identical to what Paul referred to as *helps* in 1 Corinthians 12:28.

John Chrysostom (AD 349–407) wisely said that "every spiritual work is a ministry," and he was completely accurate in that assessment. While not everyone is called to be a preacher, every member of the Body of Christ is called to be a servant or a minister in the biblical sense of the word. While its root specifically refers to a recognized position within the church, *deaconing,* in principle, could loosely refer to any type of serving in the Lord's work, and the activities that could fall under this description are almost limitless.

In the churches I visit, I am constantly amazed at the wonderful volunteers who work with children and youth, who greet and usher, who clean the building and visit the sick. Others work in areas such as food distribution, nursing home ministry, parking lot and media teams, and so forth. The areas in which vital contributions are made seem endless. These individuals might never preach behind a pulpit, but their gifts to the health and ministry of the church are of incalculable worth.

Many exalt pulpit ministry, and while it is most certainly important, it is not necessarily more important in God's eyes than what may appear to others to be the humblest of tasks. Jesus is our supreme example in this. He not only demonstrated a servant's heart by washing the feet of his disciples and going to the cross for us all, but he communicated Heaven's value system when he said:

> *Kings and those with great authority in this world rule oppres-*
> *sively over their subjects, like tyrants. But this is not your calling.*
> *You will lead by a completely different model. The greatest one*
> *among you will live as the one who is called to serve others,*

because the greatest honor and authority is reserved for the one with the heart of a servant. For even the Son of Man did not come expecting to be served but to serve and give his life in exchange for the salvation of many (Matthew 20:25–28 TPT).

I can only assume that Martin Luther King Jr. had the above passage in mind when he said, "Everybody can be great because anybody can serve."

Giving

...If it [your gift] *is giving, give generously...* (Romans 12:8 NLT).

Some might find it unusual that Paul indicated there is a special grace—a gift of giving in which believers can operate. After all, aren't all believers supposed to be giving people? I believe that is exactly correct, that all children of God are to be generous, but it seems that some people have a special grace for giving, just like some have a special grace enabling them to teach or preach. This would be an above-and-beyond-the-ordinary type of giving.

For example, a gentleman came to me many years ago at a church service and asked if he could share something with me. He proceeded to tell me he had been conflicted for several years because he had sensed a call to serve God but had no interest or desire to preach. He felt being called was synonymous with becoming a preacher, and he couldn't harmonize the two in his own life. After hearing some teaching on these passages in Romans 12, he realized that people could be graced in other areas besides speaking.

He and his wife discussed this, and they realized that they had always loved giving. As a matter of fact, the offering was their favorite part of every church service (how many people do you think can say that?). They saw *giving* listed as one of the operations of grace in Paul's teaching and were inspired to really channel their efforts to excel in this area. They recognized that ten percent—the tithe—was like a basic Christian responsibility, and they decided to increase their giving incrementally over the years ahead.

He shared with me that they then set a goal to give twenty percent to the Lord, and they had achieved that the previous year. After this they had revised their goal to giving thirty percent of their income for that current year and living on the remaining seventy percent. He said they were actively trusting God for wisdom and increase, but they were on track to achieve that as well. He said their plan was to increase their giving an additional ten percent each year until they were giving ninety percent of their personal income to the Lord and living off of ten percent of their income.

What impressed me from what this man shared was not the numbers or the potential dollar amounts, but the joy with which he shared what God had put on their hearts. No one told them to do this. No one was pressuring, manipulating, or even suggesting to them to engage in this type of generosity. They were simply acting from the grace of God at work in their hearts and from the leadership of the Holy Spirit.

Another outstanding example of the grace demonstrated through giving pertains to the Green family, the founders of the Hobby Lobby corporation based in Oklahoma City. Today, Hobby Lobby is the largest privately-owned arts-and-crafts retailer in the world with locations in forty-seven states and employing more than 43,000 people. This all began in 1970 when David and Barbara Green took out a $600 loan and began making miniature picture frames in the garage of their home.

In spite of humble beginnings, the Greens have demonstrated extravagant generosity for decades. Every year their target is to give away approximately half of their company earnings and to use the other half of their profits toward growing the business. Green states his strong belief:

> That we are put on this earth to give, to devote ourselves to a radical brand of generosity that changes lives and leaves a legacy. To paraphrase God's words to patriarch Abraham, we are blessed so that we can be a blessing.... Since I have been exceptionally blessed in my life, I have determined to give exceptionally as well.... God has taught me that with great wealth and power comes great obligation to the next generation.[13]

Green's words have been put into practice, with the company giving hundreds of millions of dollars to various Christian causes through the years.

Ironically, Green felt like the black sheep of his family since he was the son of a Pentecostal pastor and the only one of his siblings who did not "go into the ministry." He writes,

> I'd been taught that people with callings became preachers and missionaries. There was no category in our theology for people who were called to "secular" pursuits, like business. Now, though, I realize that a man can be as called to business as any preacher has ever been called to the ministry.[14]

Though Green did not become a preacher like his father, the generosity that was consistently modeled by his parents made a profound and life-long impact on him.

Because of their love for God, Walter and Marie Green often gave large portions of their modest weekly salary back to the church and also gave generously to missions. Green's mother crocheted and sold doilies so she could also give personal offerings to missions. It was this kind of godly influence that caused Green to begin tithing (giving ten percent to the Lord) as a grade schooler with the money he earned picking cotton.

This spirit of generosity that began with the giving of pennies has since evolved to hundreds of millions of dollars being funneled into the work of the Kingdom of God and the advance of the gospel. Green's position and purpose is clear: "If we don't use Hobby Lobby's earnings to touch people for the Lord, I really don't see the reason for me to be in business at all."[15] When it comes to giving, what you and I do may not be near the magnitude of what the Green family does, but what an inspiration it is for all of us to be generous and fully committed to the advancement of God's work in the earth.

This Kingdom financing mentality described in the previous stories reminds me of two different expressions of extravagant giving found in Scripture. I thought of the group of women who helped underwrite much of what Jesus did in his ministry. Luke wrote of some women Jesus had ministered to who sometimes traveled with him and the twelve. He stated that these women and *"many others…were contributing from their own resources to support Jesus and his disciples"* (Luke 8:3 NLT). Also, in the early days of the church in Jerusalem, we read, *"There were no needy people among them, because those who owned land or houses would sell them and bring the money to the apostles to give to those in need"* (Acts 4:34–35 NLT). Thank God for people who give joyfully and sacrificially because of their love for him and his work.

If someone reads this and begins to feel guilt or pressure, he or she should remember that we all have *"gifts differing according to the grace that is given to us…"* (Romans 12:6 NKJV). As with this gift, and any other gift or grace or ministry, we are not all called or equipped to do the same thing. Not everyone is going to be led by God to give ninety percent of their income to God's work. We should not feel superior if we have a particular gift, nor should we feel inferior because of the grace in which someone else operates.

We would do well here to remind ourselves of what Paul taught the Corinthians:

> *Yes, the body has many different parts, not just one part. If the foot says, "I am not a part of the body because I am not a hand," that does not make it any less a part of the body. And if the ear says, "I am not part of the body because I am not an eye," would that make it any less a part of the body? If the whole body were an eye, how would you hear? Or if your whole body were an ear, how would you smell anything? But our bodies have many parts, and God has put each part just where he wants it. How strange a body would be if it had only one part! Yes, there are many parts, but only one body. The eye can never say to the hand, "I don't need you." The head can't say to the feet, "I don't need you." In fact, some parts of the body that seem weakest and least important are actually the most necessary* (1 Corinthians 12:14–22 NLT).

Thank God for his wise distribution of gifts and graces throughout the church!

Leading

> *…If God has given you leadership ability, take the responsibility seriously…* (Romans 12:8 NLT).

A good argument could be made for me to have put leadership in the first category of this chapter, under "those who speak." After all, leadership is often expressed through words. It is not uncommon for leaders—pastors and others—to operate proficiently in prophecy, teaching, and exhortation as described earlier in this chapter. I have included leading in this latter section, though, because leaders often influence through other avenues, including their example, their foresight, and a strong gift of faith.

Those who exercise leadership often have a sense of God's plan and direction, and they influence others accordingly. Godly leaders think far more about their responsibilities from and before God than they do their authority relative to people and organizations. Similarly, many people look at leaders and think of their privileges without recognizing their pressures.

Leaders usually have a strong sense of what *could be* and what *should be,* and they channel their efforts to bring people along on a journey toward such destinations. Leaders are often big picture people, and they don't necessarily do well with details. Often, God will lead managers—detail-oriented individuals—to assist visionaries. Likewise, he often will join relationship-oriented individuals with task-oriented people. If people with different strengths like these can learn to respect each other's gifts and perspectives, powerful teams can be built. It is vital, though, that their gifts be used in a complementary way.

Henry and Tom Blackaby write:

> The New Testament indicates that Christ purposed for His followers to be a royal priesthood and a kingdom people with a common purpose and a common Lord. The body of Christ is comprised of interconnected and interdependent units (churches) that function within the reality of a larger kingdom. God expects His people to work with one another in unity and harmony and will give them one heart and one mind to serve Him together. God never intended His people to compete with each other in His kingdom, but to complement one another in their work.[16]

Not all leaders are what we would call senior leaders. Some operate like the Roman centurion who told Jesus, *"I am under the authority of my superior officers, and I have authority over my soldiers..."* (Matthew 8:9 NLT). At times these assistants are acting as a subordinate, while at other times they are directing those under their supervision.

Do Leaders Need Training?

I have had the privilege of teaching church leaders and workers for many years, and it is something I greatly enjoy. I have often seen leadership teaching called into question based on the fact that, in some translations, the word *servant* is used a massive amount, while the word *leader* is rarely used. Someone asked, "The word *leader* is referred to only six times in the Bible (KJV), while the word *servant* is used hundreds of times! Why do we have so many leadership conferences?"

I wondered if the implication behind that question is that teaching on leadership is somehow unimportant, misguided, or perhaps unscriptural. There are some important things to consider here. First, it can be very misleading to present an idea simply based on the number of times a word is used in the Bible. The statement indicates that the word *leader* only appears six times in the Bible. The assumed inference in that statement is that because of the word's infrequent usage, leadership (or leadership teaching) must not be all that important.

However, the low occurrence of the word *leader(s)*, as cited in that particular comment, is only correct in the King James Version. In the New King James Version, the word *leader(s)* is used on 116 occasions. When you check the New Living Translation, the words *leader(s)* and *leadership* are used 542 times. That's a big jump from six!

It is also essential to realize that other New Testament words besides *leader* capture the *concepts* involved in leadership. For example, *overseer, pastor, shepherd, elder,* and *bishop* all have relevance to the exercising of leadership in the church. In 1 Corinthians 12:28, Paul also referred to *administrations* (NKJV) or *governments* (KJV). Likewise, the Old Testament refers many times to people in leadership positions without necessarily using the term *leader.* In these cases, words like *king, ruler, prince, shepherd, judge, captain,* and *elder* are used instead.

Along these same lines, it is vital to realize that the importance of a *concept* is not necessarily determined by the frequency of the usage of a given *word.* For example, do you know how many times the word *Trinity* is used in the Bible? The correct answer is zero; the word *Trinity* is not found in the Bible. Does this mean that the Trinity is, therefore, unimportant? Absolutely not! The *concept* of the Trinity is revealed through a myriad of references to the Father, Son, and Holy Spirit throughout the New Testament. Are we to conclude that the triune nature of God is not important because the word *Trinity* does not appear in the Bible?

To carry this illustration to an absurd level, one could also write: "The word *Trinity* never appears in the Bible. *Satan, devils,* and *evil spirits* are mentioned 185 times (KJV)! Why do we have so much teaching about God?" Clearly, such a statement is ludicrous, but it is the same type of logic reflected in the leadership/servanthood argument referenced earlier.

Further, I believe people often miss important truths in Scripture because they look at things from an either/or perspective instead of a both/and viewpoint. In other words, nowhere does God say, "Choose ye this day which ye shall have—an attitude of servanthood *or* better leadership skills." The two concepts are not mutually exclusive; they should work hand in hand. Every spiritual leader *should* operate with a servant's heart. Servanthood and spiritual leadership are no more mutually exclusive than the fact that Jesus is both the Lamb of God *and* the Lion of the Tribe of Judah.

It has often been said that "ministry is people business," and that is very true. Beyond *senior* leaders, anyone who manages, supervises, or influences people can benefit by increasing and sharpening their leadership skills. Whether we call them directors, department heads, coordinators, supervisors, or assistants, many people lead, and they will typically lead better if they have quality training and instruction.

The reality is that the Bible is absolutely loaded with guidelines and principles for godly leadership. Those who were selected to assist Moses in ministering to the people of Israel were to be *"capable, honest men who fear God and hate bribes"* (Exodus 18:21 NLT). If those were necessary characteristics in leaders, isn't it reasonable to believe that Moses probably taught about those traits at times?

MOSES AND THE TRAINING OF LEADERS

Long before Israel had a king, Moses gave instructions for the ones who would fulfill that important role in Israel.

> *You are about to enter the land the LORD your God is giving you. When you take it over and settle there, you may think, "We should select a king to rule over us like the other nations around us." If this happens, be sure to select as king the man the LORD your God chooses. You must appoint a fellow Israelite; he may not be a foreigner. The king must not build up a large stable of horses for himself or send his people to Egypt to buy horses, for the LORD has told you, "You must never return to Egypt." The king must not take many wives for himself, because they will turn his heart away from the LORD. And he must not accumulate large amounts of wealth in silver and gold for himself. When*

he sits on the throne as king, he must copy for himself this body of instruction on a scroll in the presence of the Levitical priests. He must always keep that copy with him and read it daily as long as he lives. That way he will learn to fear the LORD his God by obeying all the terms of these instructions and decrees. This regular reading will prevent him from becoming proud and acting as if he is above his fellow citizens. It will also prevent him from turning away from these commands in the smallest way. And it will ensure that he and his descendants will reign for many generations in Israel (Deuteronomy 17:14–20 NLT).

Moses provided godly wisdom on what leaders (kings) were not to do, as well as what they were to do. All of that certainly sounds like leadership instruction to me.

As we move further along in Scripture, we see that David's final words on earth include these instructions concerning the nature of godly leadership. *"The God of Israel said, the Rock of Israel spoke to me: 'He who rules over men must be just, ruling in the fear of God'"* (2 Samuel 23:3 NKJV).

For the hearts of leaders to remain right, a reverential fear of God must operate in their lives.

JESUS AND THE TRAINING OF LEADERS

When Jesus came on the scene, he recruited disciples who would ultimately serve as witnesses of his resurrection. Jesus prepared them for the significant leadership responsibilities that would eventually come upon them, emphasizing godly values and principles that were to be implemented as they carried out their tasks. Jesus often corrected his disciples when their attitudes or actions did not represent him or the Father properly.

When Jesus spent time with his disciples, he wasn't just making profound statements so they would be enlightened. Rather, he was teaching them such practical things as:

- This is how we do ministry, and this is how we don't do ministry.

- This is how we treat people, and this is how we don't treat people.

- This is how we represent Heaven, and this is how we don't represent Heaven.

In short, Jesus was training them to have a common mindset and a shared culture concerning how ministry was to be done. He regularly coached them on what he considered to be the core values of having the right attitude and approach toward ministry.

Consider these cases in which Jesus was essentially telling his disciples, "We don't do ministry that way; we do it this way." These are all examples of leadership training.

- Mark 10:13–14: The disciples rebuked those who brought little children to Jesus. The Lord admonished them to stop restraining the children and to allow them to come to him.

- Luke 9:49–50: John told others to stop casting out demons in Jesus' name because they were not part of the twelve. Jesus told them not to do that and encouraged John to look at others as allies, not adversaries.

- Luke 9:54–56: James and John wanted to call down fire from Heaven to destroy a village because they refused to welcome the Lord. Jesus rebuked them and reminded them he had come to save people, not destroy them.

- Luke 10:17–20: The twelve celebrated their authority over demons, but Jesus told them to rejoice instead that their names were written in Heaven.

- John 21:20–22: Jesus told Peter how he would eventually die and said, "Follow me." Instead, Peter looked at John and said, "What about him?" Jesus essentially told Peter to mind his own business—not to worry about John—and to simply follow him.

- Matthew 16:21–23: When Jesus said he had to go to Jerusalem and be killed, Peter took him aside and rebuked him. Jesus responded, "Get thee behind me Satan." Peter quickly learned that it was not his job to tell Jesus how to run his ministry.

Perhaps Jesus' definitive statement on leadership is found in the following verses.

> You know that the rulers in this world lord it over their people, and officials flaunt their authority over those under them. But among you it will be different. Whoever wants to be a leader among you must be your servant, and whoever wants to be first among you must become your slave. For even the Son of Man came not to be served but to serve others and to give his life as a ransom for many (Matthew 20:25–28 NLT).

Rather than dismissing the need for leadership training, Jesus highlighted key virtues—such as servanthood, a sacrificial mentality, and a giving nature—that reflect the nature of God in leading others. In the same stroke, Jesus rejected fleshly, carnal approaches to leadership.

PAUL AND THE TRAINING OF LEADERS

As we move further in the New Testament, we see Paul conducting a leadership meeting in a "retreat" venue in nearby Miletus with the elders from the church in Ephesus. I encourage you to read (slowly) Paul's admonitions to these church leaders in Acts 20:17–38. Paul presented the example of his own life and ministry to demonstrate how they were to serve Christ. He presented such vital topics as humility, consecration, perseverance, and doctrinal content, and he also provided details about the serious nature of their God-given responsibilities.

In addition to holding personal meetings with elders (church leaders who were responsible for feeding the flock and exercising spiritual oversight), Paul also wrote Timothy and Titus very powerful letters that are referred to as the pastoral epistles. These letters are replete with all kinds of instruction as to how these two younger ministers were to carry out their spiritual assignments. Paul encouraged Timothy and Titus to discharge their duties with humility, boldness, perseverance, and wisdom. In essence, the pastoral epistles represent leadership training in the form of a letter.

Over the years, I have heard people refer to *doctrine* in a very negative tone (e.g., "We don't want any doctrine around here"). Likewise, I have heard people speak disparagingly of *theology*. The truth of the matter is that doctrine and theology are not problematic in and of themselves; what's bad is *bad* doctrine and *bad* theology. In the same way, leadership teaching must be judged on its actual content. I don't want *bad* leadership teaching either! But done well, doctrine, theology, and leadership instruction are vital and helpful tools.

WHERE DOES THIS BRING US?

Perhaps some have heard leadership teaching that discounted scriptural principles or negated the importance of prayer, caring for people, and reliance upon the Holy Spirit. I would have a problem with that also. But should we throw out the baby with the bathwater? Unfortunately, those who think in all-or-nothing terms have a tendency to do that. Of course, we are to be discerning. I was taught early in my ministerial training to "eat the hay and spit out the sticks." If the substance of leadership teaching is biblical, promotes Christlikeness, expounds upon scriptural principles, and equips pastors and others to lead and serve more effectively and with greater wisdom, I'm all for it. Church leaders need all the help they can get as they guide their congregations and promote the spiritual growth of believers in these challenging times.

MERCY

> *...And if you have a gift for showing kindness to others, do it gladly* (Romans 12:8 NLT).

In a world that is full of heartache and pain, the need for those who are powerfully moved by God's mercy and compassion is great. It is important that we declare God's Word, because people need the truth. It is also important that we demonstrate God's mercy, because people have a desperate need to sense his love flowing toward them. The psalmist wrote that *"Mercy and truth have met together..."* (Psalm 85:10 NKJV). This is important, because we don't want mercy without truth, nor do we desire truth without mercy.

Mercy is such a vital part of God's nature toward us, and without mercy, it is unimaginable that any of us could be saved. Jeremiah wrote,

"The faithful love of the LORD never ends! His mercies never cease. Great is his faithfulness; his mercies begin afresh each morning" (Lamentations 3:22–23 NLT).

The Psalms are full of cries and appeals for mercy, and throughout Jesus' ministry, people were constantly calling to him for mercy, especially when it came to people who were in need of healing or deliverance.

As much as we see people beseeching God and Jesus for mercy throughout Scripture, Jesus made a startling statement in Luke 6:36, *"Therefore be merciful, just as your Father also is merciful"* (NKJV). The New Living Translation renders that same passage, *"You must be compassionate, just as your Father is compassionate."* This brings us to one of the most powerful and dynamic truths in the New Testament: We are not just called to be consumers of God's blessings; we are called to be distributors! We are not just called to be recipients of God's mercy and compassion; we are called to be transmitters of the same! Jesus commanded his earliest disciples to *"Give as freely as you have received!"* (Matthew 10:8 NLT). This applies to us just as much as it applied to them.

I'm not sure how impressed Jesus is with every sermon that is preached in his name, but I feel confident that he values every act of mercy and compassion that his children display. We may think it's always the big things that get God's intention, but Jesus said that if you *"give even a cup of cold water to one of the least of my followers, you will surely be rewarded"* (Matthew 10:42 NLT). Mercy and compassion are huge to God! As a matter of fact, Jesus described the actions of the sheep (as opposed to those of the goats) when he judges the nations in this way:

> For I was hungry, and you fed me. I was thirsty, and you gave me a drink. I was a stranger, and you invited me into your home. I was naked, and you gave me clothing. I was sick, and

you cared for me. I was in prison, and you visited me' (Matthew 25:35–36 NLT).

Those who were commended did not recall when they had ministered to Jesus in such ways, and he told them, *"I tell you the truth, when you did it to one of the least of these my brothers and sisters, you were doing it to me!"* (Matthew 25:40 NLT).

It is in this same spirit that Mother Teresa said:

> I see Jesus in every human being. I say to myself, this is hungry Jesus, I must feed him. This is sick Jesus. This one has leprosy or gangrene; I must wash him and tend to him. I serve because I love Jesus.

When I first heard this statement by Mother Teresa, I had difficulty with it. I was so used to thinking of Jesus being triumphant and reigning in majesty. I simply could not picture "sick Jesus." And in reality, Jesus certainly is not sick, but when we recognize how much he, in his compassion, identifies with those who are hurting—how he is touched with the feelings of our infirmities—we can begin to understand how he said that when we do it to the "least of these," we are doing it to him.

It is important to recognize that we have a basic Christian responsibility when it comes to mercy. All of us are to show mercy. However, some people are especially gifted and graced in this area, and their demonstrations of mercy are very important.

These mercy-gifted individuals are like Dorcas in Joppa. Luke wrote that she *"was always doing kind things for others and helping the poor"* (Acts 9:36 NLT). When she died and Peter arrived, the *"room was filled with widows who were weeping and showing him the coats and other clothes Dorcas had made for them"* (Acts 9:39 NLT). Mercy was not a mere feeling or thought she had toward people; this beautiful spiritual attribute showed up in tangible works and expressions of kindness.

Jesus told the story we often refer to as the Good Samaritan. When the Samaritan came across an individual who had been robbed and wounded, *"He felt compassion for him...soothed his wounds with olive oil and wine and bandaged them. Then he put the man on his own donkey and took him to an inn, where he took care of him"* (Luke 10:33–34 NLT). Jesus commended this Samaritan and told his disciples to emulate his actions.

Likewise, Paul expressed heartfelt appreciation for a man who showed him mercy and kindness during some of his darkest hours.

> *May the Lord show special kindness to Onesiphorus and all his family because he often visited and encouraged me. He was never ashamed of me because I was in chains. When he came to Rome, he searched everywhere until he found me. May the Lord show him special kindness on the day of Christ's return. And you know very well how helpful he was in Ephesus* (2 Timothy 1:16–18 NLT).

Those who operate in high levels of mercy beautifully reflect the very heart of Jesus. After all, he is the one who was moved with compassion when he saw the hurting multitudes (see Matthew 9:36).

THINK AND DISCUSS

1. How does Paul's statement in Romans 12:4 (*We have many members in one body, but all the members do not have the same function*) relate to you and other believers you know?

2. Does it seem clear to you that different people can operate at different levels or degrees of grace in these areas? For example, someone might be graced to teach a small group of believers, while another might be graced to teach multitudes. Should we think more highly of one person simply because their reach is more extensive or because the scope of their ministry is larger? Why or why not?

3. This chapter dealt with seven gifts or expressions of God's grace found in Romans 12:6–7.

   - Prophecy
   - Ministry (Serving)
   - Teaching
   - Exhortation
   - Giving
   - Leading
   - Mercy

   a. Which of these do you think you are most graced in relative to your service of God and his people?

b. Which of these would you consider to be "secondary graces"? By this, I mean they may not be your primary strength, but you still sense a God-given aptitude in an area.

c. Which of these particular graces do you feel are not strong areas for you?

d. Beside each of the gifts listed above, think of or write the names of an individual or two you know of who functions well in that particular area.

CHAPTER FIVE

GIFT-MIXES, TERMINOLOGY, AND OTHER EXPRESSIONS OF GRACE

*Every Christian, then, should be vitally concerned with and per-
sonally interested in what the Bible tells us about the functions of
the members. These functions—called gifts in the Bible—are special
abilities. They are gifts from God out of the store of His grace. Paul
wrote to the Roman church this reminder:*

*"For I say, through the grace given unto me, to every man that is
among you, not to think of himself more highly than he ought to
think; but to think soberly, according as God hath dealt to every man
the measure of faith" (Romans 12:3).*

*Paul then makes it plain that all believers in the church had been
given "gifts differing according to the grace that is given to us" (12:6).*

—A. W. Tozer [17]

In the previous chapter, we discussed God's grace being expressed through
believers in prophecy, serving, teaching, exhortation, giving, leading, and
mercy. As I read that list in Romans 12, I can't help but think that Paul did
not mean that list to be excessively rigid or exhaustive. In other words, I
believe it was a representative list, kind of a "for example" list. It seems to
me that there could be many other expressions of grace that Paul could

have listed here. However, he gave enough to help us realize that grace has been given to help us serve God and others in a wide variety of ways.

For example, just a few verses later, Paul told his audience, *"...Always be eager to practice hospitality"* (Romans 12:13 NLT). This term can mean "the love of strangers." Is it possible that hospitality is just as much an expression of God's grace as prophecy, teaching, and the others? Similarly, immediately before Peter told his audience about believers being graced to speak or to serve, he admonished them, *"Be hospitable to one another without grumbling"* (1 Peter 4:9 NKJV).

In discussing the cover of this book, I mentioned Pastor Steve Smothermon. (He's got the sign in his church that says, "An empty seat is a serious matter.") Steve relates a story from decades ago when he and his wife, Cindy, were looking for to a church to attend.

The church they visited was meeting in an industrial park, and some of the buildings were spread out a bit. They had parked and were standing in front of one of the buildings with their three children. A lady saw them and realized they did not know where to go. Even though she had a walking cast, was carrying a young child on her hip, and appeared to be eight or nine months pregnant, she asked if she could help them.

This helpful lady personally escorted Steve and Cindy to two separate buildings so they could drop off their kids at the appropriate classrooms, and then she led them to the sanctuary. After they were seated, a friendly usher came over and visited with them, adding to their sense of feeling welcomed. Before the service ever started, before a single song had been sung, and before they had even seen or heard the pastor, Cindy said to Steve, "Based on how friendly and kind the people are here, I think this is where we should attend church." Steve agreed, and that became their church home for many years. This is the power of hospitality—of loving strangers and making others feel welcome!

Another reason I am inclined to think the list in Romans 12 was not meant to be exhaustive is because of other listings that Paul gave. In a later chapter, we will explore Paul's reference to the fivefold ministry—apostles, prophets, evangelists, pastors, and teachers—from Ephesians 4:11. Likewise, in 1 Corinthians 12:8–11, Paul listed numerous other manifestations and expressions of the Holy Spirit.

- Word of wisdom

- Word of knowledge

- Faith

- Gifts of healings

- Working of miracles

- Prophecy

- Discerning of spirits

- Different kinds of tongues

- Interpretation of tongues

Shortly after this, Paul noted, *"God has appointed these in the church: first apostles, second prophets, third teachers, after that miracles, then gifts of healings, helps, administrations, varieties of tongues"* (1 Corinthians 12:28 NKJV).

In examining the lists in Romans 12, 1 Corinthians 12, and Ephesians 4, it is apparent that they all vary somewhat from each other. There is some overlap in some of the lists, and it would be my guess that in some cases, Paul uses different terminologies to describe what might be the same essential gifts. For example, it seems plausible that *serving* (in Romans 12) might be the same as or at least very similar to *helps* (in 1 Corinthians 12). And it does not seem to be a big stretch to think there might at least be some overlap between *leaders* (in Romans 12), *administrations* (in 1 Corinthians 12), and *pastors* (in Ephesians 4). Depending on the situation, these gifts probably overlap some, but in other cases, I'm sure they have distinctions. Either way, I don't think we need to be overly rigid or dogmatic about it.

GIFT-MIXES?

Peter Wagner is the first person I heard use the term *gift-mix*. He wrote:

> Many Christians are multigifted. I would suspect that probably the majority of Christians, or perhaps even all, have what we could call a gift-mix, instead of just a single gift. Given the variety of spiritual gifts, the degrees of giftedness in each personal case and the multiple ministries through which each gift can be exercised, the particular combination of these qualities that I have been given and the combination that you have been given may be the most important factor in determining our spiritual personalities.[18]

Can you imagine the limitless number of combinations that might exist when you consider the various lists given in the New Testament? Imagine a pastor with a strong teaching gift in addition to strong leadership or administration gifts. How very different that pastor might be than one who has more of an evangelistic gift combined with strength in the areas of exhortation and mercy.

And then think of believers who are not called to pulpit ministry, but are strongly graced in serving, mercy, and helps. Their service for God would be expressed differently than either of the pastors mentioned above, but what a great blessing they will be to their church and to many individuals. Another person who is graced to serve might not be all that mercy-oriented, but he or she might be highly gifted in the area of technology, computers, and media. It takes all kinds of people with all kinds of gifts and abilities to meet the vast needs of the church and the world!

Not Exclusive

We discussed earlier that these listings were not meant to be *exhaustive*, but to give us an idea of many of the ways God's grace might enable us to serve. It is also important to understand that these lists were also not meant to be *exclusive*—they were not meant to box us in and keep us from serving God in practical ways or from fulfilling basic Christian responsibilities.

For example, let's say I've read through all of these Scriptures, have noted my own inclinations, and have determined that I am called to teach. If I am sitting in a church service and the pastor mentions that at the conclusion of service all of the chairs need to be stacked against the wall because of a youth event that evening, is it alright if I pitch in and help because there is a need and I am able to help? Or should I think through the Romans 12 list and say to myself, "You know, I'm called to be a teacher, therefore I should not get out of my calling by serving. I'm just going to let those called to serve move those chairs"?

That may seem like a somewhat ridiculous illustration, but I wonder how many people over the years have passed up simple opportunities to help because something was "not their calling." We should remember Paul's admonition, *"Therefore, as we have opportunity, let us do good to all, especially to those who are of the household of faith"* (Galatians 6:10 NKJV). Perhaps serving in practical ways (as described in Romans 12) may not be my primary calling, but it is good for me to take any opportunity I have to serve others. Many times, that is simply an expression of walking in love. Do you really need a "special calling" to be helpful in simple, practical ways?

Similarly, if someone comes up to me and asks me to forgive them for something, it would be highly inappropriate for me to say, "I'm sorry, but I don't have the gift of mercy described in Romans 12. Teaching is my gift." No, mercy—in the sense of forgiving someone—is not the gift described in Romans 12. Rather, it is a basic Christian responsibility. Please don't use "I'm not called" or "That's not my gift" as cop-outs from displaying Christian character, walking in the love of God, or exhibiting the fruit of the Spirit. We do many things in life just because we are God's children; they don't involve a special calling.

Imagine this line of thinking in the context of a natural family. When I was growing up, my parents expected me to help with chores just because I was part of the family. My mom taught my brothers and me to do all kinds of housework, including ironing, sweeping, dusting, and so forth. Let's say I had great skill in carpentry (which I didn't) and could help with special woodworking projects around the house. When it was time to clean the kitchen, it would not have gone well if I'd said, "Mom, I'm only gifted in carpentry, so I'm not going to help with drying the dishes."

While I never said that to her, I did on occasion tell her I wasn't good at what she was asking me to do. She never said, "Oh, Tony, you only have to help in areas where you are gifted." Actually, she told me on more than one occasion when I complained about a task I disliked, "You just need more practice." It's great when we can do what we are gifted to do, but sometimes we just need to roll up our sleeves and help because we are part of the family.

WHAT ABOUT PRAYER?

Being a *pray-er* or *prayer warrior* is not specifically listed among the gifts or ministries in Paul's listings, and yet we would all affirm strongly that prayer is absolutely vital to the health and welfare of the Body of Christ. Is it possible that Paul might have considered the ministry of prayer to fit under the area of *helps* that he described in 1 Corinthians 12:28 or *serving* as mentioned in Romans 12:7? Prayer certainly helps others, and it is a beautiful way of serving.

Some have noted that we do not necessarily see Jesus teaching his disciples how to preach in the four Gospels, but we do see him teaching them to pray. In one of Jesus' most challenging moments, the agony of Gethsemane, Jesus did not seek a sermon or Bible lesson from his disciples, but he requested their partnership and support as he prayed.

> *Then He came to the disciples and found them sleeping, and said to Peter, "What! Could you not watch with Me one hour? Watch and pray, lest you enter into temptation. The spirit indeed is willing, but the flesh is weak"* (Matthew 26:40–41 NKJV).

Jesus was praying in preparation for the cross, but he also admonished Peter to pray in the light of the stringent test that his leading disciple would imminently face.

It is remarkable how often the New Testament describes the absolute necessity and efficacy of prayer throughout its pages. We often think of the great prayers offered by leaders throughout the Bible, but the following verses highlight regular, ordinary, day-to-day believers praying, along with instructions they were given concerning prayer.

All the believers lifted their voices together in prayer to God.... After this prayer, the meeting place shook, and they were all filled with the Holy Spirit... (Acts 4:24,31 NLT).

Peter was therefore kept in prison, but constant prayer was offered to God for him by the church (Acts 12:5 NKJV).

Keep on praying (Romans 12:12 NLT).

You are helping us by praying for us. Then many people will give thanks because God has graciously answered so many prayers for our safety (2 Corinthians 1:11 NLT).

Pray in the Spirit at all times and on every occasion. Stay alert and be persistent in your prayers for all believers everywhere (Ephesians 6:18 NLT).

Devote yourselves to prayer with an alert mind and a thankful heart. Pray for us, too, that God will give us many opportunities to speak about his mysterious plan concerning Christ... Pray that I will proclaim this message as clearly as I should (Colossians 4:2–4 NLT).

Pray without ceasing (1 Thessalonians 5:17 NKJV).

Finally, dear brothers and sisters, we ask you to pray for us. Pray that the Lord's message will spread rapidly and be honored wherever it goes, just as when it came to you. Pray, too, that we will be rescued from wicked and evil people, for not everyone is a believer (2 Thessalonians 3:1–2 NLT).

Therefore I exhort first of all that supplications, prayers, intercessions, and giving of thanks be made for all men, for kings and all who are in authority, that we may lead a quiet and peaceable life in all godliness and reverence (1 Timothy 2:1–2 NKJV).

In every place of worship, I want men to pray with holy hands lifted up to God, free from anger and controversy (1 Timothy 2:8 NLT).

Pray for us... (Hebrews 13:18 NKJV).

Confess your sins to each other and pray for each other so that you may be healed. The earnest prayer of a righteous person has great power and produces wonderful results (James 5:16 NLT).

This type of praying is for every one of us —for every believer. When we cooperate with the Holy Spirit in prayer, God uses us to make a difference.

How many can testify that they are only alive because someone prayed for them, or have only had fruitfulness and effectiveness in their lives because someone lifted them up and kept them lifted up before the Lord? Paul seems to have deeply valued the prayers that believers offered for his safety and the effectiveness of his ministry.

Countless spiritual leaders have also remarked on the significance and centrality of prayer as God's work is carried out in the earth. Consider the following statements:

We cannot all be leaders, but we can all be pleaders; we cannot all be mighty in rhetoric, but we can all be prevalent in prayer.
—Charles H. Spurgeon

We are not told that Jesus ever taught His disciples how to
preach; but He taught them how to pray.
—D. L. Moody

What the church needs today is not machinery or better,
not new organizations or more and novel methods, but men
whom the Holy Spirit can use—men mighty in prayer. The
Holy Spirit does not flow through methods, but through men
of prayer. And we might add, through women of prayer.
—E. M. Bounds

Prayer does not fit us for the greater work;
prayer is the greater work.
—Oswald Chambers

The western church has lost the prayer stamina of the
mission churches in Asia, Africa, South America, Indonesia,
and those of the underground church in many parts of the
world. Yes, we are great organizers, but poor pray-ers.
—Paul E. Billheimer

When we work, we work; but when we pray, God works.
—Max Lucado

Praying is a constant reminder that we are not alone and that we have
a mighty partner who is omnipotent.

SPURGEON AND PRAYER

Some of the most effective spiritual leaders throughout history have been both proponents and practitioners of fervent prayer. The story is frequently told that when Charles Spurgeon welcomed visitors to the massive Metropolitan Church sanctuary, he would often ask them if they wished to see the "boiler room" of the church. They typically thought he was referring to an actual furnace room, but when he opened the door, a hundred or more of the church members would be on their knees, crying out to God.

Spurgeon was called "The Prince of Preachers," and yet he valued prayer tremendously and, in essence, said that prayer did not take a back seat to preaching. Addressing the priestly work of believers in a message entitled, "A New Order of Priests and Levites," Spurgeon remarked:

> And where the service has not taken the form of preaching, we can remember some whom God hath made eminent in prayer. Never account prayer second to preaching. No doubt prayer in the Christian church is as precious as the utterance of the gospel. To speak to God for men is a part of the Christian priesthood that should never be despised.[19]

Spurgeon not only esteemed prayer in general, but he greatly valued believers praying for him personally. After describing the pressures and responsibilities he faced in pastoral ministry, Spurgeon stated, "I make an especially earnest, personal appeal for my own self. I crave, beyond all things, your constant prayers."[20] As Spurgeon's success increased, he never forgot his sense of reliance on the spiritual support he received from his congregation. He said, "I have always, with my whole heart, and without any sort of untruthfulness, ascribed all the success I ever had to the prayers of God's people, and I unfeignedly do the same now."[21]

Spurgeon also called upon believers to recognize the pressing need for prayer if the church is to cooperate with God in the fulfilling of his purposes:

> How could we look for a Pentecost if we never met with one accord, in one place, to wait upon the Lord? Brethren, we shall never see much change for the better in our churches in general till the prayer-meeting occupies a higher place in the esteem of Christians.[22]

Similarly, he said:

> But when we have done all that we can, let us pray much more than we ever have done. Oh, for a praying church! I rejoice that ever since I have been with you, the spirit of prayer has never died out amongst us and I earnestly entreat you never to let it do so. May our prayer meetings be sustained in fervor and increased in number! Praying is, after all, the chief matter. Praying is the end of preaching. Preaching has its right use, and must never be neglected, but real heart devotion is worth more than anything else. Prayer is the power which brings God's blessing down upon all our work.
>
> I beg you, day by day, as you walk the streets, to have this petition in your hearts and in your mouths, "'Cause thy face to shine upon thy sanctuary.' O God, bless Your church all over the world—in Europe, in America, in Asia, in Africa, in Australia! Everywhere prosper Your work among the heathen, and in our own highly favored land too, cause your face to shine upon your sanctuary." And do not cease to present that prayer until, to the fullest possible extent, it shall be answered. And when will that be? When He comes, for whose coming we look with joyful expectation. The Lord blesses you for Christ's sake! Amen.[23]

Spurgeon so believed in the vital role of prayer that he encouraged the bedridden to realize how much they could accomplish and how much they could help through their prayers. He said, "Amazing possibilities lie within the reach of the believing man."[24]

FINNEY ON PRAYER

Charles Finney (1792–1875) was one of the greatest evangelists in American history, and God used him mightily in what is often referred to as the Second Great Awakening. Finney himself was a man of prayer, and he remarked, "Unless I had the spirit of prayer, I could do nothing."[25] However, his ministry also benefitted greatly from specific prayer partners who labored with him, not in a public or visible way, but behind the scenes in powerful intercession. Of Abel Clary, Finney said:

> He had been licensed to preach; but his spirit of prayer was such, he was so burdened with the souls of men, that he was not able to preach much, his whole time and strength being given to prayer. The burden of his soul would frequently be so great that he was unable to stand, and he would writhe and groan in agony.... He never, that I could learn, appeared in public, but gave himself wholly to prayer.[26]

Finney continued, speaking of "the wonderful spirit of prayer that was upon" Clary and said, "He was a very silent man, as almost all are who have that powerful spirit of prayer."[27]

Another who often assisted Finney in prayer was Daniel Nash, who was affectionately referred to as Father Nash. When Finney learned of his passing, he remarked, "Beloved Father Nash prayed himself away to the throne."[28] The epitaph on his tombstone reads, "Laborer with Finney.

Mighty in Prayer." Finney could not have agreed more, neither could he have been more appreciative for the spiritual support he received from his partner in ministry.

Finney had seen a remarkable transformation in Nash's life, and in his autobiography, Finney described his friend in the following ways:

> He was full of the power of prayer. He was another man altogether from what he had been at any former period of his Christian life. I found that he had a praying list, as he called it, of the names of persons whom he made subjects of prayer every day, and sometimes many times a day. And praying with him, and hearing him pray in meeting, I found that his gift of prayer was wonderful, and his faith almost miraculous.
>
> Father Nash, as we called him, who in several of my fields of labor came to me and aided me, was another of those men that had such a powerful spirit of prevailing prayer.
>
> I did the preaching altogether, and Brother Nash gave himself up almost continually to prayer...
>
> Father Nash... rose up, as his custom was, at a very early hour; and went back to a grove some fifty rods, perhaps, from the road, to have a season of prayer alone. It was before sunrise; and Brother Nash, as usual, became very much engaged in prayer.[29]

Finney also described one situation where the revival work was facing severe opposition and seeking God through prayer was their response. According to Finney, he and Nash:

> ...decided that this opposition must be overcome by prayer, and that it could not be reached in any other way. They therefore retired to a grove, and gave themselves to prayer until

they prevailed, and were confident that no power which earth or hell could interpose would be allowed to stop the revival.[30]

Clary and Nash were not the only ones who worked with Finney in prayer. In his reflections on the Rochester revival, often thought to be the high-water mark of Finney's work, he mentioned the highly influential work of numerous intercessors. "The spirit of prayer was poured out powerfully, so much so, that some persons stayed away from the public services to pray, being unable to restrain their feelings under preaching."[31]

Another great leader in the church, Andrew Murray (1828–1917), called believers to recognize the untapped power and potential that is available in the arena of prayer:

> Who can say what power a church could experience if it gave itself to prayer day and night for the coming of the kingdom, for God's power on His servants and His Word, for the glory of God in the salvation of souls? Most churches think their members are brought together to take care of one another and build each other up. Often they are unaware of the fact that God rules the world by the prayers of His saints, that prayer is the power by which Satan is conquered, and that by prayer the church on earth has authority over the powers of the spirit world. They do not fully realize, if they know it at all, that Jesus has by His promise consecrated every assembly in His name to be a gate of heaven, where His presence is felt and His power is experienced.[32]

Murray also said, "It is your highest privilege as priests of God to be intercessors."[33]

THINK AND DISCUSS

1. What do you think of the idea of people having a gift-mix or being multigifted? What would you say is your dominant gifting from God? Are there some secondary gifts you believe you have also been given to use in your service to God and others? Who are some people you know who have a blend of gifts, and how do you see them operating in these?

2. Can you think of times when you have served others, not according to a particular gift you have received but simply in fulfilling a basic Christian responsibility? What are some of the things you do, not because of a specific calling but just because they are good and appropriate things to do?

3. Re-read the list of Scriptures on prayer beginning on page 98. Without being judgmental of others, how strong do you believe your prayer life is, and how many of those admonitions are you practicing in your life? What steps can you take to increase the effectiveness of your prayer life?

4. Charles Spurgeon spoke of how much he craved the prayers of his people, and he attributed all of his success as a pastor to the prayers of his congregation. Do you think pastors today are prayed for as much as they are criticized?

CHAPTER SIX

HOW JESUS SAW MINISTRY

Ministry is pretty simple. Love people and help them.

—T. L. Osborn

When I was a young Bible School student, one of our instructors repeatedly directed us to a powerful verse describing Jesus' ministry: *"Then Jesus went about all the cities and villages, teaching in their synagogues, preaching the gospel of the kingdom, and healing every sickness and every disease among the people"* (Matthew 9:35 NKJV). He would then emphasize that Jesus did three primary things in his ministry: teach, preach, and heal. He drilled that into us and would often ask us, "What three things did Jesus do in his ministry?" In unison, all of the students would enthusiastically respond, "Teach, preach, and heal!"

THE MINISTRY OF THE WORD AND THE SPIRIT

We might also refer to this threefold emphasis as the ministry of the Word and the Spirit. So many verses throughout the Bible talk about Jesus' ministry of teaching and preaching. People *"marveled at the gracious words which proceeded out of His mouth"* (Luke 4:22 NKJV), and *"The people were astonished at His teaching, for He taught them as one having authority"* (Matthew 7:28–29 NKJV). Jesus' ministry was comprised not only of words, but of action as well. Peter said, *"God anointed Jesus of Nazareth with the Holy Spirit and with power,"* and that he *"went about doing good and healing all who were oppressed by the devil, for God was with Him"* (Acts 10:38 NKJV).

Due to my narrow view of ministry, I associated those three elements exclusively with ministry from the pulpit. It is easy to understand associating teaching and preaching with the pulpit, but at that time (four decades ago), a healing line followed pretty much every sermon in the services I attended. People would flock to the front to have hands laid on them for healing (see Mark 16:18; Luke 4:40). These prayer lines were always in the area in front of the pulpit, so I associated this with pulpit ministry as well. In my mind, what happened in and around the pulpit was the be-all and end-all of ministry.

It is not surprising then, when I became an assistant pastor shortly after this, that I saw pulpit ministry as the crown jewel of church work. I still greatly value the ministry of the Word and the Spirit, but at that time, I failed to place proper value on the many aspects of ministry that occur outside of and away from the pulpit. When the senior pastor went over my initial job description with me, I was disheartened that teaching, preaching, and healing were nowhere to be found. Instead, he wanted me to follow-up on first-time visitors, assist in pastoral care, oversee the benevolence program of the church, and develop outreach ministry.

I did what I was asked to do, but in my immaturity, I felt that I was engaging in activities that were somehow less significant than, and inferior to, pulpit ministry. Over time, the pastor began allowing me to teach classes and even speak in the church services, mostly on Sunday and Wednesday evenings, but occasionally, I was privileged to preach on Sunday mornings. Anytime I was teaching and preaching, I felt like I was on the mountaintop—doing ministry that *really* mattered. I was faithful in my other tasks, but I never saw them as being on the same level as what I did in the pulpit.

By the time I resigned from that position, I had been preaching quite regularly. After I gave my farewell sermon, the pastor graciously encouraged the people to come and wish Lisa and me well regarding our new direction. In a split second, I vainly imagined what people might say as they bid us farewell. I envisioned people thanking me for all of the sermons and Bible lessons I had shared with them, and I dared to think that some would tell me how drastically my preaching of God's Word had changed their lives.

What actually happened, though, was both surprising and sobering to me. In spite of all the sermons I had preached, not one person said thank you for anything I had done from the pulpit. Instead, people thanked me for all kinds of interactions I had had with them. For example:

- One person said, "Thank you for the time that you came and sat with us at the hospital while our daughter had emergency surgery. It meant so much that you prayed with us and kept us company until the doctor came out and told us everything was alright."

- A gentleman expressed appreciation for me calling him to my office when I heard he had lost his job. He reminded me that I had not only given them food to help him and his family during that time, but that I had also given him the names and phone numbers of some business owners in the church who might be able to help him in his search for new employment.

- Another conveyed gratitude that I had met him and his wife at the funeral home when his mother had died, and I helped walk them through the arrangement process. He also

mentioned that I had come to their home after the funeral
and had made other follow-up calls in the weeks and months
after his mother's death.

These expressions seriously challenged my preconceived ideas concerning what was really important about ministry. I know that pulpit
ministry is important; I don't value it less than I ever have. What changed
was a drastic increase in my appreciation for other aspects of ministry
beyond the pulpit. I know that people benefit when the Word of God is
preached, but what people mentioned following that service were *pastoral*
and *relational* aspects of ministry. They were expressions of care targeted
directly to their needs at critical times in their lives.

So, what was I going to do now with Matthew 9:35? I certainly didn't
appreciate it less, but I had to realize there was more to vital ministry than
pulpit and pulpit-related ministry. My instructor had taught the verses
that follow Matthew 9:35 as well, but for some reason, I had only locked
on to the part about teaching, preaching, and healing. Now it was time to
appreciate the verses that followed, the verses I had failed to appreciate.

We know that Jesus ministered with optimum effectiveness. He had
the Spirit without limit (see John 3:34 NLT). Who could have ever taught
or preached as proficiently as Jesus? Who had a greater anointing for healings and miracles? In my mind, I thought that every person throughout
Israel would have had all of their needs met and would have been spiritually flourishing after hearing Jesus minister, but is that what happened?
No doubt multitudes were blessed as Jesus taught, preached, and healed,
but Jesus himself indicated that many needs were yet to be met.

PASTORAL (OR RELATIONAL) MINISTRY

The very next verse reads, *"When he saw the crowds, he had compassion on them because they were confused and helpless, like sheep without a shepherd"* (Matthew 9:36 NLT). Wait a minute! These people were in the same areas where Jesus had just ministered. These people lived where Jesus had just taught, preached, and healed, but Matthew says they were confused and helpless. The Amplified Bible renders it this way: *"...They were bewildered (harassed and distressed and dejected and helpless), like sheep without a shepherd"* (AMPC). Don't forget to notice the compassion that moved Jesus here. He loves people and wants to see their deepest needs met.

As important as teaching and preaching are, Jesus did not say the people needed more sermons and Bible lessons. As important as prayer for the sick and hurting can be, Jesus did not say the people needed another prayer line. He said they were like sheep without a shepherd! The words *shepherd* and *pastor* in the English language are translated from the exact same Greek word. Those who minister with a pastor's heart know their flock and live with the people.

Jesus provided some very basic descriptions of how a pastor cares for and ministers to the flock. For example:

- *"The sheep recognize his voice and come to him..."* (John 10:3 NLT).

- *"...He calls his own sheep by name and leads them out"* (John 10:3 NLT).

- *"After he has gathered his own flock, he walks ahead of them, and they follow him because they know his voice"* (John 10:4 NLT).

- *The shepherd's "purpose is to give them a rich and satisfying life"* (John 10:10 NLT).

- *"...The good shepherd sacrifices his life for the sheep"* (John 10:11; see also John 10:15 NLT).

We also learn that a shepherd, in contrast to the hireling, won't abandon his sheep when the wolf comes, because he really cares about the sheep (see John 10:12–13). The idea here is that a shepherd continues with his flock; he is with them in good times and bad.

Further, a good shepherd knows his sheep and is known by his sheep (see John 10:14). Through these passages, we learn that a pastor doesn't just preach a sermon, teach a Bible lesson, or pray a prayer for people. He or she may certainly do all of those things, but there is a much deeper element of really continuing with the flock, leading them, and knowing them. In no way am I undermining the significance of teaching and preaching, but pastoral ministry means that we don't just give people a message; we give them our hearts. I am thankful for every form of ministry. Big meetings certainly have their place, but so do times of personal, relational ministry in one-on-one situations and other smaller settings.

Of course, there is the pastoral *office*—those who are called to lead and superintend an entire congregation. But in countless churches, many others are present who have a pastoral *heart*—people who are spiritually mature and highly relational. They work alongside their pastor in caring for the people, encouraging the discouraged, and walking with people through the challenges and pressure of life. Such personal care does not take the place of the oversight provided through the pastoral office, but it certainly supplements it in a most wonderful way. Relational ministry can convey the same vital truths that are shared from the pulpit and communicate and express them in a personal and meaningful way.

THE MULTIPLICATION OF LABORERS

I hope I'm not reading too much into this, but it appears that the passages we've looked at so far present two dimensions of ministry: (1) the ministry of the Word and the Spirit, which includes teaching, preaching, and healing, and (2) pastoral or relational ministry. Overlap exists between these two areas, but I think the distinction is helpful. Jesus wasn't finished yet though. *"Then He said to His disciples, 'The harvest truly is plentiful, but the **laborers** are few. Therefore pray the Lord of the harvest to send out **laborers** into His harvest'"* (Matthew 9:37–38 NKJV).

Here Jesus used another term, *laborers*. This certainly includes those who engage in teaching, preaching, healing, and pastoral forms of ministry, but I would propose that the term *laborers* can include a broader category of Christian workers. For a church to be healthy and thriving, it needs dozens, if not hundreds, of non-preaching workers for every single person who speaks from behind the pulpit.

William Godbey (1833–1920) was a powerful evangelist in the Wesleyan holiness movement. In commenting on 1 Corinthians 12:28, he wrote:

> Oh! the infinite value of the humble gospel helpers! Thousands of people who have no gifts as leaders are number one helpers, and beat the preachers working in the audience and at the altar. How grandly revival work moves along when red-hot platoons of fire-baptized helpers crowd around God's heroic leaders of the embattled host. Efficient leaders are indispensable in the Lord's work. Though we cannot do without them, yet we do not need many. We need a hundred flaming helpers to one revival leader. Hence the Lord gives us just about that proportion. If He makes you a leader of His embattled host, give Him glory; if you are only an humble

helper, shout the louder, remembering that it was Jonathan's armor-bearer who put to flight the Philistine army. The Holy Ghost is more humble than any of us, and He is our Armor-Bearer, verifying the office of the most humble helper on the battlefield. Lord, help us to accept His situation, and there abide, with the constant shout of gratitude![34]

Godbey recognized that some would exert their influence from the pulpit, while others would work "in the audience and at the altar." In other words, he was drawing attention to the importance of those who work with people one-on-one.

The ratio that Godbey proposes—one hundred helpers for every one leader—is interesting. People tend to focus so much on the preacher and forget all of the noble and honorable people working behind the scenes who make the church work and who make ministry possible. In the same chapter Godbey was referencing (1 Corinthians 12), the apostle Paul spoke of the church as a body. In that analogy he referred to hands and feet as well as eyes and ears. Paul didn't specifically refer to mouths per se, but we've all heard of preachers referenced as God's mouthpiece. When you think about it, though, the mouth makes up a very small percentage of the overall body. Also, many parts of the body can do many things that the mouth cannot do.

Please note that Jesus made this statement about laborers in the context of prayer. He specifically told his disciples to *"pray the Lord of the harvest to send out **laborers** into His harvest"* (Matthew 9:38 NKJV). Do you think Jesus would have told his disciples to pray for something he had not prayed for? Before Jesus selected the twelve, he prayed all night long (see Luke 6:12). They were laborers, of course, and when we say *yes* to Jesus, we become laborers as well. In doing this, we literally become an answer to Jesus' prayer! Laboring for the Lord is not a small thing.

What Does the Work of Laborers Look Like?

Jesus commanded all of his disciples to *"love one another; as I have loved you, that you also love one another"* (John 13:34 NKJV). No Christian is exempt from this. It stands to reason, then, that we are all called to ministry, because love (biblically speaking) involves action. John admonished believers, *"Dear children, let's not merely say that we love each other; let us show the truth by our actions"* (1 John 3:18 NLT). The Passion Translation renders that same passage, *"Our love can't be an abstract theory we only talk about, but a way of life demonstrated through our loving deeds."*

People have a tendency to only classify "big things" as ministry, such as the work of a missionary or pastor, but Jesus made it clear that he recognizes and appreciates the seemingly small works done in his name, including those that are subtle and behind-the-scenes. For example, the Lord said there is a reward for simply giving a little one who is a disciple a cup of cold water (see Matthew 10:42). Jesus praised the generous heart of the widow woman who put two small coins in the collection box (see Mark 12:41–44 NLT). Further, Jesus said that the Father would reward us when we give to the poor, pray, and fast discreetly and privately (see Matthew 6:1–18).

When Jesus was on this earth, he was aware when people were engaged in loving, giving, and serving, and he notices when we do such things as well. No act of love and devotion was so small as to escape Jesus' attention. When the widow woman put two small coins in the offering, Jesus took note. He remarked, *"This poor widow has given more than all the rest of them. For they have given a tiny part of their surplus, but she, poor as she is, has given everything she has"* (Luke 21:3–4 NLT). It wasn't the size of the various gifts that Jesus focused on, but the size of people's hearts, and this woman had the biggest heart of all.

Think and Discuss

1. In this chapter, we identified three dimensions of ministry: (1) the ministry of the Word and the Spirit, (2) pastoral (or relational) ministry, and (3) the multiplication of laborers. Which of these three do you most relate to? Which ones have you received benefit from and how? Which ones have you engaged in and how?

2. Of the three categories mentioned above, identify a person (or people) you know who operates proficiently in these different categories. What is it that makes that person especially proficient?

3. Do you feel you've had a narrow view or a broad view of ministry in the past? Have you tended to exalt one form or style of ministry above others? What are some areas of ministry that you have perhaps devalued in the past that might be very important to the heart of God?

4. The description of pastoral or relational ministry talked of those who walk "with people through the challenges and pressure of life." Whether you stand in the office of the pastor or not, how much do you feel you have operated in this type of care and ministry toward others? Assuming you have done this, how fulfilling or rewarding is it to you to function this way? Is it invigorating or draining for you to engage in pastoral or relational ministry?

5. Think about the concept of *laborers* from Matthew 9:37–38 and also the comments about the multiplication of laborers in this chapter. How many believers do you know who are actively laboring for the Lord? What do you think of Godbey's suggestion that we need one hundred workers for every preacher? How is your church doing in terms of people laboring together for the health of the church and the advancement of the gospel?

CHAPTER SEVEN

THE PURPOSE OF THE FIVEFOLD MINISTRY

Every believer, the feeblest as much as the strongest, has the calling to live and work for the kingdom of his Lord. Every believer has equally a claim on the grace and power of the Holy Spirit, according to his gifts, to fit him for his work. And every believer has a right to be taught and helped by the Church for the service our Lord expects of him.

—Andrew Murray [35]

When Jesus left this earth and ascended into Heaven, he did not leave believers helpless. He sent the Holy Spirit to help us. He even made this shocking statement, *"It is to your advantage that I go away; for if I do not go away, the Helper will not come to you; but if I depart, I will send Him to you"* (John 16:7 NKJV). Clearly, Jesus did not expect the Holy Spirit to have a passive, distant role in the life of the church. One of the ways the Holy Spirit helps us is by imparting different types of graces—supernatural abilities—into the lives of the people he has chosen to fulfill certain tasks.

We examined earlier in this book how God has given grace to people to speak and to serve (see 1 Peter 4:11). In this chapter, we will focus specifically on those roles that typically involve a heavy emphasis on speaking and are often referred to as the ministry gifts of Christ or as the fivefold ministry gifts. It is important to understand that the roles Jesus and the Holy Spirit fulfill in helping the church are one hundred percent complimentary. They never work against each other in any way, and we should always be open and surrendered to both the lordship of Christ and the influence of the Holy Spirit. In this particular area, Christ may give the gift, but the Holy Spirit anoints and empowers people as they use the gift in serving.

Paul referred to specific gifts that have been given to the church by its head, Jesus Christ. Let's look at these in the context of specific questions:

1. WHO ARE THESE GIFTS?

> *Now these are the gifts Christ gave to the church: the apostles, the prophets, the evangelists, and the pastors and teachers* (Ephesians 4:11 NLT).

The gifts referred to here are not people in general. Rather, the gifts mentioned in this passage are people with specific gifts, those who have been called and anointed by God.

2. FOR WHAT PURPOSE WERE THESE GIFTS GIVEN?

> *Their responsibility is to equip God's people to do his work and build up the church, the body of Christ* (Ephesians 4:12 NLT).

Notice here that the ministry gifts are not given to do all of God's work, but rather, to equip God's people to do the work. The NIV renders this verse well, *"...to equip his people for works of service, so that the body of Christ may be built up."*

God's people are to be equipped by these ministry gifts. This equipping conveys the idea of bringing God's people to perfection (maturity), correcting what needs correction, completing what is deficient, and preparing and making them ready for works of Christian service. I cannot stress highly enough that the responsibility of the fivefold ministry is to equip God's people, not to entertain them.

The word for *equipping* (*katartizō* in the Greek) was used in the medical field for setting a broken bone. Domestically, it was used for the furnishing of a house. Vocationally, it was used of fishermen mending their nets. In each of these cases, the *katartizō* resulted in something being able to be used the way it was intended to be used, to effectively fulfill its function.

If your leg is broken and the doctor sets it in a cast so it can heal properly, the end result is that you'll be able to walk the way you were created to walk. If a room is empty, and it is furnished (through bringing in tables, chairs, etc.), then the room can be utilized as it was intended. If a fishing net has all kinds of tears and kinks, and the fisherman mends it, the net can achieve optimum success in fulfilling its intended purpose of catching fish. When we are fully equipped, we can serve God and others the way we were designed to; we become mature, functioning, and fruitful.

3. How Long Will These Gifts Be Here?

> *This will continue until we all come to such unity in our faith and knowledge of God's Son that we will be mature in the Lord, measuring up to the full and complete standard of Christ* (Ephesians 4:13 NLT).

Would anyone seriously argue that the church has reached ultimate unity and maturity, that we measure up *"to the full and complete standard of Christ*"? If not, it is imperative that we acknowledge that Christ's gifts remain in the church and that we still need their influence. We still have much growing and maturing to experience!

4. WHAT ARE <u>OTHER OUTCOMES</u> OF THE OPERATION OF THESE GIFTS?

Paul proceeded to amplify the purpose of these ministry gifts, as well as the outcomes of having them function effectively.

> *Then we will no longer be immature like children. We won't be tossed and blown about by every wind of new teaching. We will not be influenced when people try to trick us with lies so clever they sound like the truth. Instead, we will speak the truth in love, growing in every way more and more like Christ, who is the head of his body, the church. He makes the whole body fit together perfectly. As each part does its own special work, it helps the other parts grow, so that the whole body is healthy and growing and full of love* (Ephesians 4:14–16 NLT).

Paul identified, in addition to equipping believers to serve, numerous other results of the functioning of these gifts. Among these are the saints becoming mature, stable, discerning, and not easily deceived. As believers receive from the Word and the Spirit that these ministers bring, they will become more loving and more Christlike, and they will become properly related to and connected with each other.

Paul concluded the above section of Scripture by referring to each *part* doing its own special work. When each person works as he or she is supposed to, *"…It helps the other parts grow, so that the whole body is healthy and growing and full of love"* (Ephesians 4:16 NLT). How many different ways can the New Testament tell us that every believer has a part to play and a contribution to make? The world has yet to see a fully activated, fully mobilized, fully functional, fully serving church, but when it does, it will be one of the most astonishing things humankind has ever witnessed.

Donald Gee, a pioneer of the Pentecostal movement, said the following of the fivefold ministry in his book, *The Ministry Gifts of Christ*:

> These ministries come fresh from the hand of the exalted and glorified Christ at the Father's right hand in heaven. They are His own provision for the continual need of ministry in His church until she has arrived at her appointed consummation; they reveal His continued love and thought for His own on earth, even though He has 'ascended on high'; they represent His deepest wisdom in the perfection with which they fully meet her deepest needs for powerful witness without, and steady spiritual growth within.[36]

As we receive from Christ's gifts, and as we apply the Word of God they teach, the results will be world-changing and God-glorifying.

NOT EVERYBODY, BUT *FOR* EVERYBODY

Not everybody in the Body of Christ is going to be one of these gifts (apostle, prophet, evangelist, pastor, or teacher), but everybody in the Body of Christ should benefit from them. While everyone can serve God in some capacity, a person cannot randomly and arbitrarily select a particular office in which he or she desires to stand. There is most certainly an element of God's sovereignty when it comes to divine callings and assignments.

Certain statements sound good initially, but upon closer examination, they are really not true. For example, how many times do we hear the statement, "You can be anything you want to be?" What if I decide I want to be the greatest singer in the world? Can I be that just because I want to be? If you ask my wife and my kids (who are all musically gifted), they will tell you that they love me, but that I really shouldn't sing anywhere except when I'm by myself. I simply don't have the vocal apparatus or the ear to be the greatest singer in the world.

Similarly, I can't just randomly decide to be an apostle or a pastor. If God has not called me to stand in one of these (or other offices), I can aspire to it all day long, but I can't conjure up or produce the needed grace and abilities on my own. If I don't have the calling, the anointing, and the required spiritual gifts, I'm not going to serve in one of those capacities. I can't fabricate any of these elements, and regardless of what I want, if God hasn't willed it, it is not going to happen.

It is inspiring and good for people to dream and explore their potential, but it would be more realistic to tell people, "You have amazing potential, and God has given you certain gifts and abilities. If you faithfully cultivate those, you will be able to have a meaningful, fulfilling, and productive life." After all, if my life is surrendered and consecrated to God, my goal in life is not to be what I want to be, but what he wants me to be.

This line of thinking is further reinforced by what Paul taught one congregation.

> All of you together are Christ's body, and each of you is a part of it. Here are some of the parts God has appointed for the church: first are apostles, second are prophets, third are teachers, then those who do miracles, those who have the gift of healing, those who can help others, those who have the gift of leadership, those who speak in unknown languages.

Are we all apostles? Are we all prophets? Are we all teachers? Do we all have the power to do miracles? Do we all have the gift of healing? Do we all have the ability to speak in unknown languages? Do we all have the ability to interpret unknown languages? Of course not! So you should earnestly desire the most helpful gifts (1 Corinthians 12:27–31 NLT).

Let me call to your attention the source of these gifts. In Ephesians 4:11 we learn of *"the gifts Christ gave to the church,"* and here we discover that *"God has appointed"* particular gifts for specific purposes. God and Christ initiate this, not us. Further, we learn that not everyone is gifted to perform these various ministries.

DIVINE CALLING VERSUS HUMAN AMBITION

Years ago, I was preaching in a developing nation. My host shared with me that several problems had been occurring in churches there because they had become consumed with titles, and many were calling themselves apostles and prophets. Some of them probably had genuine calls to ministry, but they were pridefully claiming titles for themselves rather than pouring themselves into genuinely serving God and others. My host asked me if I could address this issue when I spoke to several hundred who had gathered for a ministers' conference.

I was glad to do that and asked that he take me to a grocery store. While there, I purchased a can of corn and a can of beans. In preparing for the message, I took the can of corn, carefully removed the bottom of the can and dumped out the contents. With the can of beans, I simply removed the label so that all people could see was a shiny aluminum can; however, the beans were still in it.

As I stood before the assembly of ministers I reached under the pulpit and produced the can with the corn label on it. I held it from the bottom so that no one could see that the can was really empty. I walked around the different sections and asked the ministers to look at the can, asking them what was in it. In every section, the ministers confidently verbalized that I was holding a can of corn.

After getting a consensus from throughout the auditorium and asking them to confirm their assessment, I rotated the can and let everyone see that the can was, in fact, completely empty. In spite of the highly visible label there was nothing inside. I told them the lesson was this: Just because a label is on the can, it doesn't mean that anything is actually inside the can.

I then went back to the pulpit and picked up the can with no label. I walked around the different sections with that can. By that time, they were suspicious that I was trying to trick them, and they wanted to see if the bottom was intact. I showed them and also let them hold it. They could tell the can contained something, but no one knew what it was. People were reluctant to guess, because they didn't want to be wrong again, and eventually I told them it was a can of beans. The point this time was: Just because a can doesn't have a label, it doesn't mean nothing is inside of it.

Then it was time for a specific application. I told them that some ministers are obsessed with labels and want everyone to call them by certain titles. I told them titles aren't necessarily wrong in and of themselves, but if pride is involved, or if that is our primary focus and concern, then something is wrong. Jesus spoke of self-promoting individuals who *"love the best places at feasts, the best seats in the synagogues, greetings in the marketplaces, and to be called by men, 'Rabbi, Rabbi'"* (Matthew 23:6–7 NKJV).

We need to focus on what God has put on the inside of us, and we need to major on delivering content and substance to the people God has placed within our sphere of influence. In other words, don't get caught up with the label, but make sure there's something good and substantive inside the can!

What Do These Gifts Look Like?

Donald Gee also provided wonderful insights about the operation of these wonderful, God-given gifts.

> One of the most charming things that meet us on the very threshold of studies on the ministry-gifts of Christ, is their wise variety.
>
> It is true that the first on the list, the apostle, seems to embrace almost every type of ministry; but there are prophets, whose ministry is inspirational and appeals to the emotional elements of human nature; and then to balance these are teachers, whose ministry is logical and appeals to the intellectual faculties. Then there are evangelists whose ministry will be almost exclusively without (outside) the church: and pastors whose ministry will be almost exclusively within the church—both equally needed and honorable.
>
> This matter of balance in ministry is vitally important to effective, aggressive ministry without, and well-rounded growth within; far more important than most believers realize. Many assemblies have no vision but that of a one-man ministry, which is expected to fulfill every requirement—evangelistic, pastoral, teaching, prophetic. One man is expected to have marked success in evangelism, be a splendid organizer, a good pastoral visitor, a competent Bible teacher, possessing in addition gifts of healing and inspired utterance. The marvel is that so many men seem to approximate at least in some measure to these exorbitant and un-Scriptural demands. Usually it is at terrific strain to themselves; and it may easily

result in their never reaching a first-class competence in what is their truly God-given line of ministry.

Other assemblies and individuals do not even seem to have the desire or vision for one man to fill every needed line of ministry; they only appear to see one line of ministry, and have neither time, nor appreciation, nor encouragement for anything beyond their own line of things. For instance, some assemblies and individual believers have no vision or enthusiasm for anything but evangelism in the narrowest sense of that term, and almost ignore teachers and teaching. On the opposite hand, there are others who would, if they had their way, have so much Bible teaching that they would turn any assembly into little more than a Bible school, and completely ignore an aggressive outside testimony.

Both the above types may quite likely unite in "despising prophesyings" (1 Thessalonians 5:20), and have no time nor place for the gifts of prophecy, tongues, or interpretation. Yet at the other extreme are those who place such an undue value and importance upon these very gifts, that they do not consider a preacher to be in the blessing and liberty of the Spirit at all unless his ministry is continually sprinkled with manifestations of this description; and they like every meeting of the assembly to be dominated by these features. In each and every case there is a serious lack of balance.

What is needed is an appreciation of the varied ministries Christ has placed in the church, and a realization that each and all of them are essential to well-rounded activity and growth. It is no uncommon thing to hear teachers disparage evangelists by calling them "superficial" or "sensational": and then to hear evangelists stigmatize teachers as being "stodgy" and "dry." Both types may unite in calling prophets fanatical and extreme; and then the inspirational folk retaliate by calling the equally God-given ministry of their brethren "car-nal" and "fleshly" when rightly understood, it is nothing of the kind. All such attitudes are wrong.

It is perfectly true that there can be extremes in evangelism which are superficial: there can be extremes in teaching which are heavy and barren: there can be extremes in prophesying which are most undeniably fanatical. Yet the true remedy is not to be found in repressing therefore any particular one of these lines of diverse ministry, for thereby we may all too easily quench the Spirit of God also. Indeed, this has been actually done too often; men have dealt with the false and unprofitable at the terrible expense of cutting out the real at the same time. It needs an inspired touch to regulate inspired ministry. The divine plan is for each and every ministry which God has set in the church to correct and complement the other, thereby providing just the elements lacking and just the check needed to restore overbalanced tendencies on any one line—the prophet to inspire the teacher, the teacher to steady the prophet; the evangelist to continually remind us of the needy world outside dying for the gospel, the pastor to show us that souls still need much caring for even after they have been "won." The apostle above all to inspire and lead the way to fresh conquests for Christ and His church.[37]

God's wisdom in giving diverse gifts for the building of his people is a stroke of genius. Some might ask, "If we are all priests, then why do we need apostles, prophets, evangelists, pastors, and teachers." I might ask in return, "If we are all citizens, then why do we need mayors, sheriffs, sanitation workers, business leaders, and school administrators?" In order for a society to operate efficiently, it needs various individuals with varying skill sets, serving the community in different ways. Likewise, in order for the church—both worldwide and on a local level—to be all that it should be, it needs many people with different abilities building God's people up and equipping them for service.

THINK AND DISCUSS

1. Reflect on these two statements from this chapter: "The ministry gifts are not given to do all of God's work, but rather, to equip God's people to do the work," and, "The responsibility of the fivefold ministry is to equip God's people, not to entertain them." What do these two statements mean to you?

2. From this chapter, did you gather that (a) the ministry gifts have been set in the church to do all of the work of the ministry, or (b) the ministry gifts have been set in the church to equip all of the saints so that each believer can do his or her part in building up the Body of Christ and fulfilling the work of the ministry?

3. What is your understanding of the following statement from this chapter? "There is most certainly an element of God's sovereignty when it comes to divine callings and assignments." Do you agree with this? Why or why not?

4. What was your impression after reading the story of the two cans? What are your thoughts on titles versus substance?

5. Put into your own words why we still need leaders and specific ministry gifts within the church even though every believer is a priest.

CHAPTER EIGHT

MULTI-DIMENSIONAL MINISTRY

The Christian that is bound by his own horizon, the church that lives simply for itself, is bound to die a spiritual death and sink into stagnancy and corruption. We never can thank God enough for giving us not only a whole Gospel to believe, but a whole world to give it to.
—A. B. Simpson[38]

I once enjoyed visiting with a person who worked in the White House, assisting the president of the United States. The stories about his responsibilities were fascinating, and one of his statements really stood out. He remarked, "There are many moving parts." He and his team did not have the luxury to just think about one responsibility or a single activity. They always had to be mindful of how what they did interfaced with many other teams, departments, and agencies who also worked for the president and his administration. The coordination among these various entities had to be seamless.

Winston Churchill also understood the idea of many moving parts. While Great Britain had one overarching purpose during WWII—to prevail in their battle against the Nazis—the war had to be fought on many fronts. In one speech, he declared:

> We shall fight in France, we shall fight on the seas and oceans, we shall fight with growing confidence and growing strength in the air, we shall defend our Island, whatever the cost may be, we shall fight on the beaches, we shall fight on the landing

grounds, we shall fight in the fields and in the streets, we shall
fight in the hills; we shall never surrender.

Having the big picture necessitated an understanding of the multi-dimensional approach it would take to win the war.

The mission that God has for his church also has many moving parts. The task he has for us is also multi-dimensional. We will address the Body of Christ as a whole, but even as individual believers, we must recognize the different tools and approaches of which God wants us to be aware. We must recognize that any one tool isn't right for every job. We must go beyond Abraham Maslow's insightful observation, "If the only tool you have is a hammer, you tend to see every problem as a nail."

We receive a basic understanding of the concept of multi-dimensional ministry when we capture the wisdom in Paul's simple statement, *"Rejoice with those who rejoice, and weep with those who weep"* (Romans 12:15 NKJV). From that, we understand that different types of ministry are appropriate at different times and in different sets of circumstances. Similarly, Paul told another congregation, *"Now we exhort you, brethren, warn those who are unruly, comfort the fainthearted, uphold the weak, be patient with all"* (1 Thessalonians 5:14 NKJV).

As we observe Jesus' ministry, we discover that he did not have a cookie-cutter or a one-size-fits-all approach when interacting with different individuals. He didn't communicate with Nicodemus the way he spoke to the woman at the well, and he didn't address the rich young ruler the way he did the woman taken in adultery. It could be argued that at the core of his ministry, Jesus always communicated an essential "believe in me" message, but the variety of strategies and styles he used reflected a multi-dimensional approach.

One of the reasons Paul's ministry was so effective is that he always maintained a singular focus (preaching Christ), and yet he operated in a diversity that clearly reflects God's wisdom. Paul's reflections on three years of ministry in Ephesus reveal the basis for much of his fruitfulness:

> *How I kept back nothing that was helpful, but proclaimed it to you, and taught you publicly and from house to house, testifying to Jews, and also to Greeks, repentance toward God and faith toward our Lord Jesus Christ* (Acts 20:20–21 NKJV).

Can you see the multi-dimensional elements in this short passage? Paul presented:

- Multi-dimensional venues (publicly *and* from house to house)
- Multi-dimensional audiences (Jews *and* Greeks)
- Multi-dimensional content (repentance *and* faith)

I don't think these complementary elements were accidental; I believe Paul operated with the wisdom of God and with a divine strategy.

We should not confuse the issue and just arbitrarily see how many things we can do and how many different ways we can do them. Sometimes ministers, believers, or churches attempt to do so many things they end up doing nothing well; they spread themselves too thin and drastically reduce their effectiveness. Much wisdom is found in this old adage: It is better to do a few things well than to do many things badly.

We should take special note of Paul's prayers for believers in his epistles. These prayers were Spirit-inspired and reflect God's will for congregations and individual believers alike. In one of these prayers, Paul wrote:

> *That Christ may dwell in your hearts through faith; that you, being rooted and grounded in love, may be able to comprehend with all the saints what is the width and length and depth and height—to*

know the love of Christ which passes knowledge; that you may be filled with all the fullness of God (Ephesians 3:17–19 NKJV).

I wonder how many believers over the centuries have read these verses without thinking about the ramifications of *"the width and length and depth and height"* of God's love that he mentioned here. Is this just a meaningless figure of speech, or does the Holy Spirit really want us to comprehend the multi-dimensional nature of God's love, and if we comprehend it, what will we do with it? How might we express it?

The Width of God's Love

When doors are open wide, it means that people are welcome to come in. When arms are wide open, it means that a person is offering acceptance and perhaps even an embrace. To say that God's love is wide essentially says the same thing. He is reaching out with open arms, welcoming all who will come to him in faith. When I think of the width of God's love, I picture Jesus saying, *"Come to me, all of you who are weary and carry heavy burdens, and I will give you rest"* (Matthew 11:28 NLT). He issued another invitation when he said, *"If anyone thirsts, let him come to Me and drink"* (John 7:37 NKJV). The width of God's love means that he has room for us and that he is inviting us to himself.

Naturally speaking, when a chair is wide, it invites us to sit in it. No one wants to be in a cramped, confined space. Years ago, when Lisa and I were ministering in an Asian country, the church auditorium had theater-type seats. I'm not speaking of the wide, spacious seats that are in many theaters today—the kind that are very well-cushioned and recline. These were the type of seats you were more likely to find in a movie theater many decades ago. After worship, Lisa and I sat down, and I immediately knew I had a problem.

The space between the two arm rests was so narrow that I immediately felt wedged into my seat. It was like I had vise grips on either side of my hips. I leaned over to Lisa and said, "I think I'm stuck in my seat. I'm not sure I'm going to be able to get up." I knew that I would be introduced to speak shortly, and I asked Lisa to put her hand on my back and push hard when it was time for me to get up. Even though my body weight had carried me deep into my seat, I was greatly relieved when my attempt to extricate myself from the chair was successful.

I remember thinking to myself: "That seat was designed for people with a smaller frame than what I have. That chair was not designed for me." God's love for us is wide in the sense that his arms are open, and we fit perfectly within his embrace. Further, his embrace is broad enough for him to welcome all who come to him in faith. In other words, the width of God's love is very relational in nature.

When believers comprehend the width of God's love and express it toward others, they will be very welcoming and will demonstrate hospitality, warmth, and acceptance. Because relationships are so important, fellowship will be a key strength of such groups. In one church, the pastor told me that a couple in his church always looked to see who the first-time visitors were on a Sunday morning. This couple would always invite at least one visitor or a visiting family out to lunch after the service and get to know them. They did this simply to demonstrate God's love and let them know they were important and welcome.

THE LENGTH OF GOD'S LOVE

If the width of God's love offers a welcome to those who come, the length of God's love reaches out to those who are far away. This "far away" can refer to those who are far away geographically or spiritually. In other words, the length of God's love is expressed through outreach, evangelism, and missions.

When Jesus directed his disciples, he told them, *"...You will be my witnesses, telling people about me everywhere—in Jerusalem, throughout Judea, in Samaria, and to the ends of the earth"* (Acts 1:8 NLT). The earliest disciples understood that their responsibilities began close to home, but Jesus' mandate would also take them far away to *"make disciples of all the nations"* (Matthew 28:19 NKJV).

We should note that the length of God's love is not simply extended to those who are far away geographically. People can be very close to us in terms of proximity, but very far away from God spiritually. This separation, or spiritual distance from God, applied to us at one time also. Paul stated, *"But now in Christ Jesus you who once were far off have been brought near by the blood of Christ"* (Ephesians 2:13 NKJV). Thank God that his love was long enough to reach us! When we think of the length of God's love, we remember the prophet's statement: *"The LORD's hand is not so short that it cannot save..."* (Isaiah 59:1 NASB).

When believers comprehend the length of God's love and express it toward others, they will be very mindful of the lost—of those outside the four walls of the church. They recognize that people are separated from God by sin and that they need to hear and receive the gospel in order to be reconciled to God. Believers express the length of God's love by giving to missions and engaging in evangelistic outreach. They value what happens inside the church amongst the saints, but they are ever mindful that *"the Son of Man came to seek and save those who are lost"* (Luke 19:10 NLT).

THE DEPTH OF GOD'S LOVE

After mentioning the width and length of God's love, Paul referred to love's depth. When something is deep, it is not shallow or superficial; it is vast and profound. Through love's width and length, God will reach out to us and offer us acceptance, but he doesn't want us to stay where we are; he ultimately wants to move us close to him and into maturity. Elsewhere, Paul taught that the Spirit of God *"searches out everything and shows us God's deep secrets"* (1 Corinthians 2:10 NLT).

When I was young and learning to swim, I was very comfortable in the shallow end of the pool. My feet could touch the bottom of the pool, so I felt at ease. After some swimming lessons, my instructors were confident I was ready for the deep end, which was twelve feet deep. I remember the apprehension I felt when the day came that they asked me to swim across what seemed like a bottomless chasm to me. Thankfully, it went well, but I never would have attempted crossing the deep end had I not had good coaching and learned the basics. Even then, it was a great comfort to know that if I experienced trouble and needed help, my teacher (also a lifeguard) was there to assist me.

Gaining confidence in the deep end of the pool opened up a new world of fun to me, mainly diving boards. I would still enjoy going back to the shallow end at times and playing with friends, but nothing compared to the exhilaration of jumping and diving from the low, medium, and eventually, the high dive. As Christians, we are also called to grow into maturity. The author of Hebrews strongly challenged his audience for their lack of development.

> *You have been believers so long now that you ought to be teaching others. Instead, you need someone to teach you again the basic things about God's word. You are like babies who need*

milk and cannot eat solid food. For someone who lives on milk is still an infant and doesn't know how to do what is right. Solid food is for those who are mature... (Hebrews 5:12–14 NLT).

In another place, Paul referred to the *"substance of our Message"* and added, *"We teach in a spirit of profound common sense so that we can bring each person to maturity"* (Colossians 1:27–28 MSG).

When believers comprehend the depth of God's love and express it toward others, they will be oriented toward growth, development, and maturity. This kind of congregation might offer various classes and discipleship opportunities to facilitate the growth of its members. Depth is not limited to knowledge, but can also include building godly character and bringing people to depth in the things of the Spirit.

The Height of God's Love

I have been in many Christian gatherings where the worship leader would admonish the people to *lift* their voice, *lift* their hands, and *lift* their hearts to God. The worship leader encouraged people to enter the heavenly Holy of Holies and to worship *the Most High God* (a term that is used more than fifty times in the Scripture). David asked, *"Who may ascend into the hill of the LORD? Or who may stand in His holy place?"* (Psalm 24:3 NKJV). Scripture also admonishes, *"Let the high praises of God be in their mouth..."* (Psalm 149:6 NKJV).

In short, God is someone we deem to be high and exalted. When we encounter God in the height-dimension of his love, he is inviting us to ascend to his manifest presence and to commune with him through praise, adoration, and worship. When believers comprehend the depth of God's love, they will worship God sincerely and with adoring hearts. Worship is not a mere preliminary, but a heart-to-heart, face-to-face encounter with the living God; it is fellowshipping with the God of the universe.

MANY MOVING PARTS

As you read the above descriptions of width, length, depth, and height, you may have found yourself asking, "Isn't the church supposed to excel, or at least have a degree of proficiency, in all of these areas?" The answer, of course, is a resounding *yes*! None of this is presented as an either/or proposition. Paul did not invite us to know the width *or* the length *or* the depth *or* the height of God's love. He wants us to comprehend all of these so we can be filled with all the fullness of God.

- When we are good at wide, we are *relational*.
  We emphasize hospitality and fellowship.

- When we are good at long, we are *missional*.
  We emphasize soulwinning and missions.

- When we are good at deep, we are *developmental*.
  We emphasize discipleship and growth.

- When we are good at height, we are *devotional*.
  We emphasize praise and adoration.

In considering all of this, we should ask ourselves, are we strong individually in all of these areas, or do we have room to grow? What about corporately? Are all of our churches proficient in all of these areas, or are some churches stronger in some areas than in others? I propose that as individuals and churches, we may grow and develop in all of these areas (and we should), but we very likely have certain strengths and inclinations that come easier to us than other areas.

For example, as a teacher, I am most inclined toward depth type of issues—things pertaining to knowledge and discipleship. When it comes to a church service, I would naturally be inclined to appreciate the sermon more than any other part. A width person might actually enjoy the fellowship before and after the service the most. That doesn't mean a width person wouldn't enjoy or benefit from the message or the worship, but they would feel the most fulfillment and satisfaction from connecting with their friends and building relationships with new people.

A height person could enjoy other aspects but would likely be most impacted by the worship and the presence of God they sense during that part of the service. Finally, a length person could enjoy all parts of the service, but nothing would compare, in his or her estimation, to leading an unsaved person to Jesus or ministering to an unreached people group.

It is important that we understand that God did not intend us to all be alike or to be clones of each other. I'm not better than anyone else, nor am I inferior to anyone else because of a particular dimension of God's love that I appreciate or walk in more intensely than another. A teacher might think that everyone should love details from commentaries or insights from church history as much as he or she does. Yet another might think that everyone should love intense, extended times of worship as much as a worshipper does. We can have personal preferences in these areas based on how we are spiritually hardwired, but we should never diminish the orientation or emphases of others.

Perhaps certain individuals or churches believe they are perfectly balanced in all of these areas. Such a person might say, "I am equally geared toward width (the relational), length (the missional), depth (the substantive), and worship (the devotional)." However, it is far more common for people—individually and corporately—to acknowledge greater strengths and weaknesses in these different areas. Many pastors have told me over the years that pulpit ministry by their preaching team was very solid, but their people were not good at connecting with or making outsiders feel welcome. Others have told me that their worship was very strong, but they were sadly deficient in their evangelistic outreaches.

Usually, a church begins by building around the pastor's primary strength or strengths. So, if the pastor is a gifted teacher, the church forms around that, and it tends to become a teaching-oriented congregation. If the pastor is highly relational, that element more easily becomes part of the DNA of that congregation. If a church is going to be multi-dimensional in its overall ministry, all the different dimensions of God's love must be acknowledged, emphasized, and celebrated. Rarely can a single individual properly lead in all of these areas.

This means that a pastor or pastoral team must identify people with different strengths and position them to lead by example. Thus, width-oriented people create a welcoming and hospitable environment in the church. Length-oriented members engage in outreach and remind the church about the lost world that needs to be reached. Depth-oriented believers lead groups in prayer and teaching and further the discipleship process among the congregation. Finally, the height-oriented saints will set a tone of heartfelt, congregational worship; some may do this from the platform, but others may simply model it from amongst the congregation.

We should never identify a particular grace or strength in our lives and assume this means that we are exempt from exercising basic Christian responsibilities. For example, I can't say, "Well, I'm a teacher, so I have no responsibilities when it comes to hospitality, outreach, or worship." I can't be unsociable toward people and justify it by saying "Width is not my gift." Neither can I stand there like a log during worship and defend my not worshipping God by saying, "I'm just not a height person." If I am geared primarily toward depth, I should allow those graces inside the width, length, and height people to inspire me and help grow me in those areas, even if none of those will ever be my primary strength. Further, I should see those other areas as being equally valuable and necessary for the Body of Christ as what I contribute.

WHAT'S IN A NAME?

I mentioned earlier that a church will often take on the primary strength of its pastor. This is especially true in the earlier stages of a church's development. For example, in the late 70s and early 80s, what many people called a *teaching revival* took place in America. Churches were starting everywhere, and a large percentage of these were really teaching centers. As a result, depth was the main emphasis for the majority of these new groups, but over time, they would recognize the need for width, length, and height, and emphasis would eventually be placed on these additional areas.

Many of these churches were named Word of Life or Word of Faith. The usage of *Word* was indicative of how much emphasis there would be on teaching the Bible. Many others actually used Teaching Center or Bible Church in their church names. In other time periods, when the emphasis in the Body of Christ was on other topics, other names would reflect length (Evangelistic Church or Outreach Center) or width (Fellowship) or height (Worship Center). Many of these churches evolved in such a way that they developed healthy, multi-dimensional ministry, but their name likely reflected a particular dimension of ministry that was one of their core values and greatest strengths at the time the name was chosen.

WHAT DO THESE DIMENSIONS LOOK LIKE PRACTICALLY?

All of these different elements can flow practically and somewhat seamlessly in a given church, but it will take many people operating with numerous graces in order for this to happen. For example, the width people can be active in greeting people (formally and informally) and expressing a sense of hospitality, acceptance, and warmth toward new and existing people alike. Even the pastor can contribute to width by using illustrations that make the Word of God understandable to the people and applicable to their lives. I remember being in one church, and during the announcements, they had a slide on the overhead screen that announced the times of various groups that met throughout the week. These included grief recovery, divorce recovery, substance abuse and addictions, as well as groups that provided instruction in budgeting and financial management issues. I remember thinking, "Wow, if I was a first-time visitor and was struggling with any of these life issues, I would want to attend a church like this that is going the extra mile to meet people at their points of greatest need."

People with a length-orientation in a congregation can mobilize formally or informally into outreach activities. Whether it is street ministry, outdoor outreaches with music and food, prison ministry, or ministry to the homeless, opportunities exist wherever lost people are found. In addition, short-term mission trips can facilitate ministry in cross-cultural settings. Many churches have a missionary department that stays in touch with missionaries that are supported by the local church. They pray regularly for the missionaries and stay in touch with them to encourage them and stay abreast of their needs. Then, prayer and financial support can be channeled to effectively support and promote ministry far beyond the four walls of the local church. It is important to remember that not everyone may be called to go to foreign fields, but all believers can be involved in praying for and sending those who are called. Finally, believers who are length oriented can pray for the church and for God's people to work effectively for the salvation of the unsaved.

People who are oriented toward the depth of God's love can first of all participate personally in the kind of growth they so deeply value. They do this by partaking of the meat of God's Word and cooperating with the Holy Spirit in prayer. While some of this may come from the pastor or other leaders in the church, the more maturity believers have, the more responsibility they have to feed themselves. It is unfortunate when mature believers expect the pastor's messages to be geared entirely toward them. The strong in the church need to celebrate when parts of the pastor's sermons are geared toward helping the lost and younger Christians, not just themselves.

Thank God for legitimately mature believers. We need such individuals in the church, especially when they guard themselves against pride. Paul explained that *"...Knowledge puffs up while love builds up"* (1 Corinthians 8:1 NIV). He also reminded believers that *"Those who are mature in their faith can easily be recognized, for they don't live to please themselves but have learned to patiently embrace others in their immaturity"* (Romans 15:1 TPT).

In addition to cultivating their own spiritual development, those who are inclined toward depth can help others grow as well. The author of Hebrews indicated that those who have had opportunities for growth should be helping others. *"You have been believers so long now that you ought to be teaching others..."* (Hebrews 5:12 NLT). Responsibility is communicated in this verse. Some will discharge the responsibility of teaching others in a group setting, leading classes or prayer groups. Others will mentor people individually.

For example, Priscilla and Aquila recognized that Apollos only had limited exposure to the things of God, so *"They took him aside and explained the way of God even more accurately"* (Acts 18:26 NLT). What did they do? They took him deeper. Shortly after this, Paul encountered twelve disciples in Ephesus and helped further their faith. After Paul baptized them in the name of Jesus and laid his hands on them, *"The Holy Spirit came on them, and they spoke in other tongues and prophesied"* (Acts 19:6 NLT).

Whether it is with an individual or a group, depth-oriented people will lead others into growth and maturity. By their example and by their words, they will help others progress and develop spiritually. They fulfill Jesus' directive by helping to make disciples. While width people provide relational warmth and length people seek the salvation of the lost, depth people focus on bringing those who have been welcomed and saved into a deeper walk with the Lord.

And finally, there are the height people. These individuals are most known for their adoration and devotion to the Lord. They worship God from the heart whether they are helping lead from a platform or are simply *"in the midst of the assembly"* (Psalm 22:22 NKJV). Height people remind us that our spiritual journey is not just about connecting with people or growing in knowledge—it is ultimately about connecting with God, exalting him, and giving him glory as he deserves. Height people are mindful of the presence of God, and they influence others toward the praise and worship of the Most High God.

AM I LIMITED TO JUST ONE?

There may be one area of service that you enjoy greatly and that you find most fulfilling. That's great, and that's likely a strong area of grace or gifting in your life. However, most people probably have more than one area in which they are anointed to serve God effectively. In the world of entertainment, some people are described as a *triple threat.* This means they are able to act, sing, and dance. Fred Astaire was considered a great triple threat in Hollywood, and ironically, the story is told of an early critic who allegedly said of the legend, "Can't sing. Can't act. Balding. Can dance a little."

Fortunately, Astaire persevered and became one of the greatest figures in the American entertainment history. Perhaps someone has spoken critically of you in a way that would suppress and discourage you from fulfilling your potential. It is possible that some areas are not your greatest strengths, and that's OK. However, don't let your gifts be quenched just because someone misjudged you or failed to see the gifts in your life.

I have been presenting these different facets as though each person is simply one of these or another. The reality is, most people are likely a blend of these—width, length, depth, and height—with one or two of these traits being more dominant in their lives. A few might say that they possess, in some measure, all four of these. However, I think most believers would say that while they appreciate all four of these dimensions, they are graced to be more highly proficient in one or two of these more than the others.

This brings us to the wisdom of God and the beauty of Christ's Body. God has not asked any one of us to do everything, but he has asked all of us to do our part. Because different ones in the church have different strengths, we can celebrate what others bring to the table. We are to complement one another and appreciate the fact that others are gifted where we are not. We are not in competition with one another; rather, we complete one another. Paul told the Ephesians that if we comprehend these four dimensions of God's love and if we *"know the love of Christ which passes knowledge,"* then we will be *"filled with all the fullness of God"*

(Ephesians 3:19 NKJV). God wants to both reveal himself and express himself fully through his church, and he does this through us.

In his classic book, *The Purpose Driven Church*, Rick Warren noted the multidimensional nature of church growth and identified various areas where churches need to grow. I modified and adapted his list slightly.[39] My adjusted list indicates that churches need to grow:

- Warmer through fellowship
- Deeper through discipleship
- Richer through worship
- Stronger through serving
- Healthier through generosity
- Larger through evangelism

One person cannot accomplish all of this, but it can happen when members of the Body of Christ with different gifts act upon the graces that God has placed in their hearts.

We would all be wise to learn from what Rick Warren observed about America's greatest evangelist, Billy Graham:

> I learned from Graham to build your ministry on a team. Graham knew this, and he built a core team that was with him 50 years. Everybody on the team brought strengths to the table. When you build an effective team, you hire people who compensate for your weaknesses and who mobilize or reinforce your strengths, because nobody can be good at everything.[40]

Whether we are leaders or team members, we can all be an integral part of God's multidimensional love being expressed in the earth.

THINK AND DISCUSS

1. Consider Maslow's statement: "If the only tool you have is a hammer, you tend to see every problem as a nail." Have you ever been one-dimensional in your perspective of ministry in the local church? How has your view changed or evolved over time?

2. What lessons can we learn from considering how Jesus dealt with various people differently, in recognizing that he did not take a cookie-cutter or one-size-fits-all approach? How do these lessons apply to our lives and to our work for God?

3. When it comes to expressing the different dimensions of God's love, which one are you most graced to do? Which do you feel is your greatest strength? Use the following list to identify your primary strength, your secondary strength, etc. Mark these from 1–4 with one being your highest.

   a. _____ Width

   b. _____ Length

   c. _____ Depth

   d. _____ Height

4. Have you ever tried to operate in one of these areas where you are not particularly graced? Maybe you are an introvert who was asked to be a greeter. What was that like for you? Do you think it's OK to sometimes step into a role just to meet a need until someone else can fill that position?

5. Identify a person (or people) you know who particularly excels in these four areas. Consider and describe the contribution that each of them make to your church.

    a. Width: _____

    b. Length: _____

    c. Depth: _____

    d. Height: _____

CHAPTER NINE

BUILDING UPON THE THREE GREATS

So necessary to the Church is a lofty concept of God that when that concept in any measure declines, the Church with her worship and moral standards declines along with it. The first step down for any church is taken when it surrenders its high opinion of God.

—A. W. Tozer[41]

Unless the church has a sharp and intentional focus, it can easily drift into non-essentials and areas that are not reflective of what Jesus intended his church to be. If the church is to rise to its potential in these crucial times, it must do so under the direction of Jesus, its glorious head, and under the direction and guidance of the Holy Spirit. The activities of the church cannot be based on human cleverness or on the energy of the flesh. In order for the church to arise God's way, it must be based upon his directives and priorities and carried out according to his revealed truth. With this in mind, let's examine three pillars upon which our identity and our assignment rests. We are going to call these *The Three Greats*.

The Great Commitment

You may not have heard this term before. When many Christians hear the word *commitment,* they likely think of messages they have heard in the past in which they are admonished to be committed to God, committed to the Bible, committed to church attendance, etc. All of these are important issues, and sermons about these topics are absolutely valid. Billy Graham noted that even Jesus spoke of and called for commitment among his earliest followers. The noted evangelist said, "Jesus didn't use subtlety or gimmicks to gain followers. Rather, He honestly laid before them the tough demands of discipleship—total commitment and total involvement."[42]

While our commitment to God is important, that is not what I am referring to in this particular section. Rather, I am referring to God's commitment to us. Our commitment to him can only be healthy and viable if we understand it to be a response to the commitment which he first made and continues to express toward us.

> *This is real love—not that we loved God, but that he loved us and sent his Son as a sacrifice to take away our sins.... We love each other because he loved us first* (1 John 4:10,19 NLT).

> *You didn't choose me. I chose you. I appointed you to go and produce lasting fruit...* (John 15:16 NLT).

The entire Christian faith rests not upon our commitment to God, but on his commitment to us. The church's commitment to the Lord may have fluctuated, faltered, and floundered from time to time, but his commitment to us has never wavered.

In communicating his commitment to us, Jesus declared, *"...Upon this rock I will build my church, and all the powers of hell will not conquer it"*

(Matthew 16:18 NLT). Jesus expressed absolute resolve in his commitment to build his church. He wasn't going to try it and see if it worked; he said he would do it. It was not a temporary experiment to be dropped if the results were not to his liking. He decreed and asserted that he would build his church, and he has never changed his mind. His resolve is further reflected in his statement, "...*And be sure of this: I am with you always, even to the end of the age*" (Matthew 28:20 NLT).

Peter articulated how he saw Jesus building his church when he told believers, "*You also, as living stones, are being built up a spiritual house, a holy priesthood, to offer up spiritual sacrifices acceptable to God through Jesus Christ*" (1 Peter 2:5 NKJV). Notice the individualistic and the corporate elements in this verse. Peter told believers that they are individually living stones, and he told them that they are corporately being built up into a spiritual house.

Allow me to repeat the essence of what I said in Chapter Two. I can walk through a field and see individual stones. They can be scattered all throughout the field, but they may be totally separated from each other. However, a skilled stone mason could gather those individual stones, cut them and fashion them according to his wisdom, and using some type of mortar, join them together into a beautiful house. That is really what the Lord does with us. Individually we are living stones, but he doesn't allow us to remain isolated and separated from each other. We are instructed to assemble together (see Hebrews 10:25); in community, we serve and partner together, allowing Jesus to build us into a spiritual house.

Paul told believers, "*Make every effort to keep yourselves united in the Spirit, binding yourselves together with peace*" (Ephesians 4:3 NLT). A stone mason makes sure that he uses a strong mortar or masonry adhesive to keep the stones connected; he doesn't want his building falling apart. Likewise, we need the strong influence of the Holy Spirit to join us and keep us connected in this spiritual house that the Lord is building.

The question is not whether Jesus will build his church; he is one hundred percent committed to that. The question is, "Will we allow him to use us, as individual stones, as the materials for his house?" If you really want to see how committed Jesus is to the building and development of his church, you need to look no further than the first three chapters of the Book of Revelation. Writing during perilous and chaotic times, the apostle John had a magnificent vision of Jesus, and he saw the Lord standing in the midst of seven golden lampstands, representing seven local assemblies of believers.

Jesus proceeded to give messages to each of the seven congregations, praising them regarding areas where they were faithful and giving them corrective guidance in areas where adjustments were needed. One thing is abundantly clear through these letters: Jesus was vitally interested in and seeking to govern every dimension of the life of these churches. John even saw Jesus walking *"in the midst of the seven golden lampstands,"* the local congregations (Revelation 2:1 NKJV).

What boldness it inspires to know that Jesus is completely committed to us and that he is absolutely dedicated to building his church. He won't quit halfway. He is not just the author, but he is also the finisher of our faith (see Hebrews 12:2). Paul told one of his beloved congregations, *"I am certain that God, who began the good work within you, will continue his work until it is finally finished on the day when Christ Jesus returns"* (Philippians 1:6 NLT). When we embrace the realization that Jesus is entirely committed to us and that his commitment is enduring, it positions us to walk in the next two *Greats*.

The Great Commission

You may be familiar with this term, which has historically been of great importance in the world of evangelicalism. But how much do modern

Christians really know about the term, *the Great Commission*? Many were shocked to read the results of a survey conducted in 2019 by the Seed Company in conjunction with the Barna Research Institute. An article based on this survey reads:

> When asked if they had previously "heard of the Great Com-mission," half of U.S. churchgoers (51%) say they do not know this term. It would be reassuring to assume that the other half who know the term are also actually familiar with the passage known by this name, but that proportion is low (17%). Meanwhile, "the Great Commission" does ring a bell for one in four (25%), though they can't remember what it is. Six percent of churchgoers are simply not sure whether they have heard this term "the Great Commission" before.[43]

Something that is truly *Great* should be known better than that, so let's explore it.

While Jesus was training his earliest disciples, it became increasingly clear that he had plans and intentions for them and for all who would follow them. He told them, for example, that they were *salt* and *light* (see Matthew 5:13–14). Such elements are influential, as salt preserves and flavors, and light illuminates. The transformative influence Jesus intended his disciples to have was further emphasized when he instructed them, *"Let your good deeds shine out for all to see, so that everyone will praise your heavenly Father"* (Matthew 5:16 NLT).

Toward the very end of each of the gospel accounts, Jesus communicated a specific sense of mission or assignment to those he had been training. The most commonly cited passages are those in Matthew and Mark.

> *Go therefore and make disciples of all the nations, baptizing them in the name of the Father and of the Son and of the Holy*

*Spirit, teaching them to observe all things that I have com-
manded you; and lo, I am with you always, even to the end of
the age* (Matthew 28:19–20 NKJV).

*Go into all the world and preach the gospel to every creature.
He who believes and is baptized will be saved; but he who does
not believe will be condemned. And these signs will follow those
who believe: In My name they will cast out demons; they will
speak with new tongues; they will take up serpents; and if they
drink anything deadly, it will by no means hurt them; they will
lay hands on the sick, and they will recover* (Mark 16:15–18
NKJV).

These were Jesus' marching orders for his church, and they remain as
such today. The Lord has never recalled his prime missional directive for
his people.

Though not as pronounced, Luke and John also recorded a sense of
this Great Commission in their gospel accounts. John wrote:

*He said, "Peace be with you. As the Father has sent me, so I
am sending you." Then he breathed on them and said, "Receive
the Holy Spirit. If you forgive anyone's sins, they are forgiven. If
you do not forgive them, they are not forgiven"* (John 20:21–23
NLT).

Central to the thought here is Jesus saying, *"As the Father has sent me,
so I am sending you."* The ramifications of that statement are profound and
far-reaching. Do we really believe that there is a similarity between the
way the Father sent Jesus and the way that Jesus has sent us? Jesus' mission
was vital to the salvation of humanity. What would have happened if Jesus
had not taken his mandate from the Father seriously? It is essential that

we treat our heavenly assignment with the same reverence and respect as Jesus did his.

Some have struggled with Jesus' statement, *"If you forgive anyone's sins, they are forgiven. If you do not forgive them, they are not forgiven."* Does this mean I can just sit in my room and say something like this? "OK, God. I now pronounce all the sins of the world forgiven," and automatically, everyone in the whole world becomes a child of God and their sins are forgiven? I don't think that's how this works. We must see Jesus' words in the overall context of the gospel.

When we preach the gospel and people believe it, they receive the forgiveness that Jesus made available through the shedding of his blood and through his death, burial, and resurrection. When Paul preached in Antioch Pisidia (in modern-day central Turkey), he said this about Jesus: *"Brothers, listen! We are here to proclaim that through this man Jesus there is forgiveness for your sins"* (Acts 13:38 NLT). Forgiveness is integrally and inseparably connected to the gospel, and the gospel must be preached.

That forgiveness is released through the preaching of the gospel is further reinforced in Paul's statement to the church at Rome:

> *Everyone who calls on the name of the LORD will be saved. But how can they call on him to save them unless they believe in him? And how can they believe in him if they have never heard about him? And how can they hear about him unless someone tells them? And how will anyone go and tell them without being sent?...* (Romans 10:13–15 NLT).

Did you catch the last part of that? Someone needs to be sent. Remember that Jesus said, *"As the Father has sent me, so I am sending you"* (John 20:21 NLT).

Luke's presentation of the Great Commission especially emphasizes the single word: *witnesses*. He recorded Jesus stating that he had fulfilled multiple prophetic statements through his death, burial, and resurrection, making forgiveness available for those who repent. Then Jesus said, *"You are **witnesses** of all these things"* (Luke 24:48 NLT). The Book of Acts picks up where Luke's Gospel leaves off, and there Luke recorded Jesus saying:

> *But you will receive power when the Holy Spirit comes upon you. And you will be my **witnesses**, telling people about me everywhere—in Jerusalem, throughout Judea, in Samaria, and to the ends of the earth* (Acts 1:8 NLT).

Again, the word *witnesses* stands out in Luke's account.[44]

In its simplest definition, a *witness* is someone who has seen or heard something first-hand. When that person testifies, he or she is not conveying hearsay, but personal knowledge. The disciples had witnessed Jesus' life, ministry, death, and resurrection, and it was their responsibility to share what they knew to be true. So profound was their experience with the Lord that when Peter and John were commanded to quit speaking about Jesus, they responded, *"We cannot stop telling about everything we have seen and heard"* (Acts 4:20 NLT).

God wants the world to know his love and his saving grace, and he expects us to demonstrate it and to make his gospel known. Jesus came to seek and to save the lost (see Luke 19:10), and his heart and intentions have not changed. God is on a mission, and he has invited us—even commanded us—to join him on his mission. Hence, it is a co-mission. Whenever you think of the Great Commission, remember that it is an activity we engage in *with* God. We are joining him in the fulfillment of his mission.

THE GREAT COMMANDMENT

Once we comprehend God's amazing commitment to us, and once we accept our responsibility to fulfill the Great Commission (not all can go, but all can pray and/or help send), we must be compelled to operate in the remarkable love of God. And this brings us to the Great Commandment. I don't know what you think of when you hear the word *commandment*, but many think of the numerous commandments issued in the Old Testament. It is commonly stated that there are 613 commandments in the Old Testament, but most people think of the Ten Commandments that were given by God through Moses.

Admittedly, it would be much easier to remember ten than the hundreds of others cited throughout the Old Testament, but one "bottom line" man approached Jesus and wanted him to identify the one commandment of greatest importance.

> One of them, an expert in religious law, tried to trap him with this question: "Teacher, which is the most important commandment in the law of Moses?" Jesus replied, "'You must love the LORD your God with all your heart, all your soul, and all your mind.' This is the first and greatest commandment. A second is equally important: 'Love your neighbor as yourself.' The entire law and all the demands of the prophets are based on these two commandments" (Matthew 22:35–40 NLT).

What a remarkable summary! Jesus encapsulated the significance of the law in two commandments that he stated are of equal importance—love God and love people.

Paul made it clear, in what is called the Great Love Chapter, that if love is not the core motivator for all we do, it is all for nothing. He wrote:

If I could speak all the languages of earth and of angels, but didn't love others, I would only be a noisy gong or a clanging cymbal. If I had the gift of prophecy, and if I understood all of God's secret plans and possessed all knowledge, and if I had such faith that I could move mountains, but didn't love others, I would be nothing. If I gave everything I have to the poor and even sacrificed my body, I could boast about it; but if I didn't love others, I would have gained nothing (1 Corinthians 13:1–3 NLT).

How sobering is that? It challenges me to make sure that I am doing things for the right reasons. I wonder how many will stand before the Lord thinking that they will receive a great prize for their labors, only to find out that their rewards were greatly reduced or entirely lost because they did things for the praise of people or for other wrong reasons? I address this issue in much greater detail in *The Work Book: What We Do Matters to God*, but suffice it to say here that we don't want to be like the person whose works fail to pass the test at the judgment seat of Christ. Paul said, *"If the work is burned up, the builder will suffer great loss. The builder will be saved, but like someone barely escaping through a wall of flames"* (1 Corinthians 3:15 NLT).

When Jesus reiterated the commandment to love, he also indicated how significant love would be in terms of our witness in the world. He told the disciples:

A new commandment I give to you, that you love one another; as I have loved you, that you also love one another. By this all will know that you are My disciples, if you have love for one another (John 13:34–35 NKJV).

Had Jesus simply instructed, "Love one another," then it would be open to interpretation as to how we would do that. But when he said we are to love one another the way he loves us, he set the standard as high as it could possibly go. It is only possible for us to do this if we truly love one another with a divine love, and this is possible *because the love of God has been poured out in our hearts by the Holy Spirit who was given to us*" (Romans 5:5 NKJV).

Further, Jesus said the love we have for and demonstrate toward one another would enable others to recognize us as his true disciples. This has been seen again and again throughout church history. One commentary remarks:

> Minucius Felix declared with regard to the Christians, "They love each other even without being acquainted with each other." And the scoffer Julian, "Their master has implanted the belief in them that they are all brethren." In his commentary on John's Epistles Jerome tells us that when John was asked by the brethren why he constantly said, "Little children, love one another," he replied, "Because this is the precept of the Lord, and if only this is done it is enough."[45]

In the middle of the second century, Justin Martyr (AD 100–165) remarked, "We who formerly hated and murdered one another now live together and share the same table. We pray for our enemies and try to win those who hate us."[46]

Another great leader in the early centuries of the church, Tertullian, made a similar statement:

> But it is mainly the deeds of a love so noble that lead many to put a brand upon us. 'See,' they say, 'how they love one another, how they are ready even to die for one another.' And they are wroth [furious] with us, too, because we call each other brethren.[47]

Believers can preach many sermons and present many rational explanations commending the Christian faith, but as these leaders have noted, demonstrations of love are powerful and persuasive tools in reaching the hearts of the lost.

One of the most prolific church historians of all time, Phillip Schaff, spoke of the powerful witness demonstrated by believers in Carthage in the middle of the third century:

> During the persecution under Gallus (AD 252), when the pestilence raged in Carthage, and the heathen threw out their dead and sick upon the streets, ran away from them for fear of the contagion, and cursed the Christians as the supposed authors of the plague, Cyprian assembled his congregation, and exhorted them to love their enemies; whereupon all went to work; the rich with their money, the poor with their hands, and rested not, till the dead were buried, the sick cared for, and the city saved from desolation.[48]

In all of these examples, believers were simply following the example of Jesus when he washed the feet of the disciples and laid his life down for us.

THINK AND DISCUSS

1. Compare and contrast your commitment to God as opposed to his commitment to you. In times when your commitment to him may have wavered, what did you discover about his commitment to you?

2. In what ways does the Great Commission (see Matthew 28:19–20; Mark 16:15–18) influence your life? In what ways does it affect your thinking, praying, giving, and actions?

3. Review the statements at the end of the chapter by Minucius Felix, Julian, Jerome, Justin Martyr, Tertullian, and the story related by Philip Schaff. Is the caliber of love coming from believers today able to have the same impact in the world as it has had in the early centuries? What can believers do in this day and age to live out the full meaning of Jesus' words in John 13:35—*"By this all will know that you are My disciples, if you have love for one another"* (NKJV)?

CHAPTER TEN

FOR SUCH A TIME AS THIS

*I shall pass this way but once; any good that I can do or any kindness
I can show to any human being; let me do it now. Let me not defer
nor neglect it, for I shall not pass this way again.*

—Etienne de Grellet, Quaker Missionary

Have you ever wondered why you were born? What about the timing of your birth? Why were you born when you were born, and even where? Perhaps your parents told you that you were unplanned, or you've had the thought that you were somehow an accident. Regardless of the natural factors surrounding your birth and your life, you were no accident to God. He has known you from before the foundation of the world, and he has both a purpose and a plan for your life.

In preaching to the Athenians, Paul stated, *"From one man he made all the nations, that they should inhabit the whole earth; and he marked out their appointed times in history and the boundaries of their lands"* (Acts 17:26 NIV). If God can mark out the appointed times of nations, what about individuals? You can believe that your life is nothing more than a coincidence of some kind, but the Bible makes clear that God has known you and has had a plan for your life even before you were born.

Consider some of the Scriptures that paint an amazing picture of God's foreknowledge and omniscience.

You saw me before I was born. Every day of my life was recorded in your book. Every moment was laid out before a single day had passed (Psalm 139:16 NLT).

I knew you before I formed you in your mother's womb. Before you were born I set you apart and appointed you as my prophet to the nations (Jeremiah 1:5 NLT).

But even before I was born, God chose me and called me by his marvelous grace... (Galatians 1:15 NLT).

...God, who has saved us and called us with a holy calling, not according to our works, but according to His own purpose and grace which was given to us in Christ Jesus before time began (2 Timothy 1:8–9 NKJV).

You are no accident, and God is not figuring things out as he goes along.

Another passage about God knowing us ahead of time and establishing a plan and purpose for our lives is what Paul wrote to the Ephesians:

We have become his poetry, a re-created people that will fulfill the destiny he has given each of us, for we are joined to Jesus, the Anointed One. Even before we were born, God planned in advance our destiny and the good works we would do to fulfill it! (Ephesians 2:10 TPT).

This is both an encouraging and sobering thought. When I read this, I am encouraged to know that I am foreknown by God and not an afterthought. God is not looking at me and trying to figure out what he is going to do with me. This verse is challenging in that I am responsible to fulfill what God has assigned me to do. I don't want to stand before him and realize that I never tapped into his plan or purpose for my life—that I did my own will throughout life, not his.

It also gives me great comfort just to realize that God knows the end from the beginning. He spoke the following through Isaiah: *"I make known the end from the beginning, from ancient times, what is still to come. I say, 'My purpose will stand, and I will do all that I please'"* (Isaiah 46:10 NIV).

Nothing is going to happen in your life or mine—or in the world at large—that is going to take God by surprise. God will never have to recall the Book of Revelation because he overestimated his ability to rule and reign through all eternity. The way God described the climax of the ages and the onset of the eternal state in the final book of Scripture is exactly the way it will transpire!

While we don't have to concern ourselves with God's ability to manage the universe and all that is within it, we should be diligent to make sure that our lives are yielded to him, his will, and his purpose. Our salvation is not based on having perfectly followed God's will; only one person (Jesus) has ever done that flawlessly. We are saved by grace through faith. However, the welfare of others can be connected to our obedience and our cooperation with him.

The story of Esther provides one of the most remarkable lessons in the Old Testament. While the Jews were in Persian captivity, an evil man named Haman tried to orchestrate the extermination of the Jewish people. At this time, a beautiful young Jewish woman named Esther had found favor in the eyes of the Persian king. Esther's uncle, Mordecai, learned of Haman's plot and realized that God had strategically placed Esther in a position where she could be used to intervene and intercede on behalf of the Jewish nation.

In coaching young Esther, Mordecai said:

> *For if you remain completely silent at this time, relief and deliverance will arise for the Jews from another place, but you and your father's house will perish. Yet who knows whether you have come to the kingdom for such a time as this?* (Esther 4:14 NKJV).

This idea of coming *"to the kingdom for such a time as this"* speaks powerfully to destiny and divine purpose. We may never have as dramatic of a moment as what Esther had, but what all of us do is important in God's overall plan. We may not single-handedly save a nation, but God can use all of us at strategic times as part of a team and in the lives of others.

Don't miss the simple opportunities in front of you every day because you are waiting for some magnificent, large-scale project. If God gives you a big assignment, great. But don't miss the small things in the meantime. Charles Dickens said, "No one is useless in this world who lightens the burden of another." Similarly, Helen Keller stated, "I long to accomplish a great and noble task, but it is my chief duty to accomplish small tasks as if they were great and noble."

If you don't have specific clarity on what you're supposed to do, find out how the Bible tells us to treat and serve one another, and look for opportunities to carry out those directives in your regular, daily life. I wrote the following in another book, and it is appropriate to repeat here:

> There are three lies in particular that the devil tells to keep you from answering God's call to become a vessel fit for His use. He tells you that if something great is going to be done, it's going to be done a) by someone different than you; b) somewhere different than where you are; and c) with gifts different than what you have. In other words, he'll tell you that great things are different, distant, and difficult.[49]

Some believers seem to have "other-itis." They say, "If certain circumstance were different, then I could serve God effectively." In a slightly different context, Paul told the Corinthians, *"And don't be wishing you were someplace else or with someone else. Where you are right now is God's place for you. Live and obey and love and believe right there"* (1 Corinthians 7:17 MSG).

To keep believers from being effective here-and-now, the accuser often tells them the following type of lies:

- God could use you if you had a better education.
- God could use you if you had a better pastor or were in a different church.
- God could use you if someone would just give you a big opportunity.
- God can only use people who are smarter than you, speak better than you, sing better than you, etc.
- God could use you if you were in full-time ministry.
- God could use you if you were younger (or if you were older).
- God could use you if you were single (or if you were married).

Another lie that the enemy tells believers is that God can't use them because they've messed up too much, because their past sin is too great.

When I consider the idea of our past sins, I think of Peter. Not only did Peter mess up, but we discover that Jesus knew ahead of time that Peter was going to fail, and he called him anyway. As a matter of fact, Jesus told him he was going to deny him, and then told him what to do after he got back on track. Your past sins did not catch God by surprise. He knew you would fail, and he loved you anyway, sent Jesus to die for you anyway, and called you to be his child anyway. Don't use this as a pretext for continuing in sin, but realize that your past does not negate God's plan for your future.

Though the Lord knew that Peter would fail, and even told him of his upcoming denial, Jesus still said, *"I have pleaded in prayer for you, Simon, that your faith should not fail. So when you have repented and turned to me again, strengthen your brothers"* (Luke 22:32 NLT). Jesus wanted Peter to know that his failure did not change God's mind. If you are being harassed because of past sin, remember that Jesus talked to Peter about repenting—about turning back to Jesus—and then re-iterated his calling and assignment.

Don't let false guilt keep you from serving God. If your past sin is haunting you, humble yourself and let God do a deep work in your heart. Allow yourself to be cleansed by the blood of Jesus and restored by the Spirit of God. If you have hurt and offended others, make sure that you have truly repented and made amends to them in whatever way you can. Don't just seek forgiveness, but seek healing for yourself and for those you have injured. Do whatever is necessary to re-earn trust and re-build credibility.

GET BUSY—NOW!

Sometimes people stress timing and preparation, and those can certainly be important. However, they should not be the basis for procrastination and neglect; they should not keep us from taking action now when we can do so. Often, serving and acting now is a major part of what prepares us to do greater things later. Others speak frequently of a great revival, a great move of God that is yet to come. That's great, but if we are doing *nothing* while we're waiting for God to do *something*, we are missing it.

Anticipation of revival should not lull us into passivity and lethargy; it should spur us to obedience and to action. I like what William Booth said, "I am not waiting for a move of God, I am a move of God!"

I am including a number of quotes from notable individuals. These have inspired me, and I trust they will encourage you as well. All of these statements communicate one imperative truth: Act!

The opportunity of a lifetime must be seized during
the lifetime of the opportunity.
—Leonard Ravenhill

"Now" is the watchword of the wise.
—Charles Spurgeon

The vision must be followed by the venture. It is not enough
to stare up the steps—we must step up the stairs.
—Vance Havner

I prayed for twenty years but received no answer
until I prayed with my legs.
—Frederick Douglass

We Christians too often substitute prayer for playing the game. Prayer is good; but when used as a substitute for obedience, it is nothing but a blatant hypocrisy, a despicable Pharisaism…To your knees, man! and to your Bible! Decide at once! Don't hedge! Time flies! Cease your insults to God, quit consulting flesh and blood. Stop your lame, lying, and cowardly excuses. Enlist!
—C. T. Studd

Opportunity is missed by most people because it is dressed in overalls and looks like work.
—Thomas Edison

Begin while others are procrastinating.
Work while others are wishing.
—William Arthur Ward

The only difference between success and failure is the ability to take action.
—Alexander Graham Bell

I am only one, but I am still one. I cannot do everything, but I can still do something; And because I cannot do everything I will not refuse to do the something that I can do.
—Edward Everett Hale

If you don't know what to do, let me encourage you to start where you are with what you have. Instead of dreaming about some far-off, future occasion, ask God to open your eyes to the opportunities that are all around you. I'm not against supernatural, dramatic leadings when God chooses to provide that, but you don't have to have a vision, dream, or audible voice to do something to serve God. Paul said, *"Whenever we have the opportunity, we should do good to everyone—especially to those in the family of faith"* (Galatians 6:10 NLT).

ARE WE IN THE LAST DAYS?

I am frequently asked if I believe we are in the last days. Theologically speaking, we absolutely are. Because Peter quoted Joel (see Acts 2:17), we can surmise that the coming of the Holy Spirit on the Day of Pentecost marked the inauguration of the last days. Some say, "But that was 2,000 years ago!" That's true. Could it be that when Peter first quoted that verse, it was the *beginning* of the last days, while today we are at the *end* of the last days? We should keep in mind that Peter also said, *"With the Lord one day is as a thousand years, and a thousand years as one day"* (2 Peter 3:8 NKJV).

Regardless of what your beliefs are concerning eschatology—whether you hold to a pre-trib, mid-trib, or post-trib rapture or have another idea altogether—the idea of the Lord's return should give us a sense of urgency and encourage us toward action. Even if you disagree with the assessment that we are in the last days described in the Bible, there is no disputing this fact: Every day that we live is *someone's* last day. Current estimates indicate that 178,000 people die each day in the world. That is 7,425 deaths each hour and 120 each minute.[50] Imagine that. Every half a second, another soul somewhere in this world passes into eternity. Did they know Jesus? Were they born again?

This is why we emphasize the urgency of the hour. This is why I am contending for every believer's involvement in ministry. This is why I am saying we must labor now. William Booth, founder of the Salvation Army, implored, "Can we go too fast in saving souls? If anyone still wants a reply, let him ask the lost souls in Hell." Similarly, Carl F. H. Henry reminds us, "The gospel is only good news if it gets there in time."

Jesus recognized the human tendency to procrastinate, put things off, and delay when he said,

> You know the saying, 'Four months between planting and harvest.' But I say, wake up and look around. The fields are already ripe for harvest. The harvesters are paid good wages, and the fruit they harvest is people brought to eternal life. What joy awaits both the planter and the harvester alike! (John 4:35–36 NLT).

Various leaders throughout history have stressed the urgency of the moment with words such as these: "If not now, when? If not here, where? If not us, who?" We would do well to re-visit those thoughts and apply ourselves diligently to the work of God at hand. We are the hands and feet of Jesus, and someone needs what we have.

THINK AND DISCUSS

1. What are your thoughts when you realize that you could have been born anywhere in the world and anywhere throughout time, but you are here where you are on this earth now? Do you believe that all of this is a coincidence, or do you believe that, like Esther, *"you have come to the kingdom for such a time as this"* (Esther 4:14 NKJV)?

2. Have you ever procrastinated or delayed when it came to serving God? What excuses did you use to justify not serving God? How did you get unstuck and get involved in serving God and others?

3. How attentive are you to opportunities around you? Can you give an example of a recent time when you took an opportunity to serve someone else? Do you ever pray for God to give you opportunities where you can be used by him in helping others?

4. Was there ever a time when you were more eager and fervent about serving God than you are now? If so, what can you do to begin rekindling your passion?

5. What does the idea of the end times mean to you? How does it affect your attitude and your actions in life?

CONCURRING VOICES ON THE PRIESTHOOD OF THE BELIEVER

If no one beyond Peter, John, and Paul had acknowledged or repeated the great themes concerning the priesthood of believer, it would still be an absolute truth. However, others throughout history have recognized this essential teaching of Scripture. For example, Justin Martyr (AD 100–165), a church father from the second century, spoke of the priesthood of all believers in these terms:

> We are the true high priestly race of God, as even God Himself bears witness, saying that in every place among the Gentiles sacrifices are presented to Him well-pleasing and pure. Now God receives sacrifices from no one, except through His priests.[51]

In the latter part of the second century, another early church leader named Irenaeus (a disciple of Polycarp who had been a disciple of the apostle John) remarked, "I have shown in the preceding book that all the disciples of the Lord are Levites and priests...."[52]

In recognizing that New Testament believers were priests, even though they came from Gentile backgrounds (and were certainly not Levites or descendants of Aaron), Justin and Irenaeus confirmed what had been hinted at in the Old Testament. Even as God chided his covenant people for their failure to honor him properly, the prophet Malachi declared:

> *"My name will be great among the nations, from where the sun rises to where it sets. In every place incense and pure offerings will be brought to me, because my name will be great among the nations," says the LORD Almighty* (Malachi 1:11 NIV).

Many scholars believe the phrase *"from where the sun rises to where it sets"* refers to a worldwide expansion of the true worship of God.

In Jesus' day, the Samaritans claimed true worship happened on Mount Gerazim, not in the Temple in Jerusalem. But when Jesus spoke to the Samaritan woman, he took the emphasis off of the location and put it squarely on the heart. He told her, *"The time is coming when it will no longer matter whether you worship the Father on this mountain or in Jerusalem"* (John 4:21 NLT).

Jesus proceeded to tell her:

> *But the time is coming—indeed it's here now—when true worshipers will worship the Father in spirit and in truth. The Father is looking for those who will worship him that way. For God is Spirit, so those who worship him must worship in spirit and in truth* (John 4:23–24 NLT).

Jesus said the emphasis would no longer be on *where* we worship but on *how* we worship. When the priestly work of the Aaronic priesthood was superseded by Jesus becoming our High Priest and every believer becoming a priest, this dynamic was realized.

Over many centuries, the church became steeped in religious hierarchy and operated less like a spiritual family. As a result, a caste system evolved that elevated select leaders and subordinated others, and tragically, ordinary believers lost their sense of priesthood. The chasm between clergy and laity was enormous.

Martin Luther (1483–1546) re-discovered certain vital truths about the rights, privileges, and responsibilities of believers as he studied the Bible during the course of his own spiritual journey. In his day, there was a rigid, distinct line drawn between clergy and laity. As his eyes were opened to the truth of Scripture, he realized that regular believers were being deprived of many of their privileges.

In his letter to the Bohemians, Luther spoke of a "spiritual and universal priesthood" of which all believers are a part. He wrote, "Indeed, all Christians are priests, and all priests are Christians."[53] He also asserted:

> That we are his brethren is true only because of the new birth. Wherefore we are priests, as he is Priest, sons as he is Son, kings as he is King. For he makes us to sit with him in heavenly places, as companions and co-heirs with him, in whom and with whom all things are given us. And many similar expressions indicate our oneness with Christ—one loaf, one cup, one body, members of his body, one flesh, bone of his bone, and we are told we have all things in common with him [Rom. 8:32; Gal. 3:28; 1 Cor. 10:17; Eph. 4:4; 5:30].[54]

Elsewhere Luther wrote:

> As Christ by His birthright has obtained these two dignities, so He imparts and communicates them to every believer in Him, under that law of matrimony of which we have spoken above, by which all that is the husband's is also the wife's. Hence all we who believe on Christ are kings and priests in Christ.

This is the inestimable power and liberty of Christians. Nor are we only kings and the freest of all men, but also priests forever, a dignity far higher than kingship, because by that priesthood we are worthy to appear before God, to pray for others, and to teach one another mutually the things which are of God. For these are the duties of priests, and they cannot possibly be permitted to any unbeliever. Christ has obtained for us this favor, if we believe in Him: that just as we are His brethren and co-heirs and fellow-kings with Him, so we should be also fellow-priests with Him, and venture with confidence, through the spirit of faith, to come into the presence of God, and cry, "Abba, Father!" and to pray for one another.

For though it is true that we are all equally priests, yet we cannot, nor, if we could, ought we all, to minister and teach publicly.[55]

Finally, Luther stated:

The priest is not made. He must be born a priest; must inherit his office. I refer to the new birth—the birth of water and the Spirit. Thus all Christians must became priests, children of God and co-heirs with Christ the Most High Priest.[56]

Luther's fellow-reformer, John Calvin (1509–1564) spoke of Christ being a priest in a class all by himself because of his redemptive work on the cross. Summarizing the teaching of Hebrews, Calvin wrote, "The priestly office belongs to Christ alone because by the sacrifice of his death he blotted out our own guilt and made satisfaction for our sins (Hebrews 9:22)."[57]

Though Calvin recognized the uniqueness of Christ's priesthood, he proceeded to elaborate on how we receive the priesthood because of our union with him.

Now Christ plays the priestly role, not only to render the Father favorable and propitious toward us by an eternal law of reconciliation, but also to receive us as his companions in this great office [Revelation 1:6]. For we who are defiled in ourselves, yet are priests in him, offer ourselves and our all to God, and freely enter the heavenly sanctuary that the sacrifices of prayers and praise that we bring may be acceptable and sweet-smelling before God.[58]

Later, Calvin reaffirmed his position on Christ's priesthood and our share in it when he wrote:

Christ was appointed and consecrated priest according to the order of Melchizedek by the Father with an oath [Psalm 110:4; Hebrews 5:6], without end, without successor [Hebrews 7:3]. He once for all offered a sacrifice of eternal expiation and reconciliation; now, having also entered the sanctuary of heaven, he intercedes for us. In him we are all priests [Revelation 1:6; 1 Peter 2:9], but to offer praises and thanksgiving, in short, to offer ourselves and ours to God.[59]

While Luther and Calvin followed Peter, John, and Paul's example in teaching the priesthood of all believers, it was Philip Jakob Spener (1635–1705) who contended passionately for "the establishment and diligent exercise of the spiritual priesthood" in the churches of his day.[60] Recognizing that regular believers had been excluded from ministry activities, including the reading of Scripture, Spener wrote:

Every Christian is bound not only to offer himself and what he has, his prayer, thanksgiving, good works, alms, etc., but also industriously to study in the Word of the Lord, with the grace that is given him to teach others, especially those under his own roof, to chastise, exhort, convert, and edify them, to observe their life, pray for all, and insofar as possible, be concerned about their salvation.[61]

In other words, Spener asserted that all believers have spiritual responsibilities throughout the course of their lives; they are called to actively participate with God as co-workers with him and with other believers.

Luther, Calvin, and Spener all recognized that Christians have different callings and graces to fulfill their respective assignments. They acknowledged that some are called to lead, to preach, etc. But they also understood that none are called to merely observe and spectate while "professional clergy" do all the work. Specifically, Spener recognized the necessary partnership among all members of the Body of Christ. Referring to all believers as priests, he wrote:

> No damage will be done to the ministry by a proper use of this priesthood. In fact, one of the principal reasons why the ministry cannot accomplish all that it ought is that it is too weak without the help of the universal priesthood. One man is incapable of doing all that is necessary for the edification of many persons who are generally entrusted to his pastoral care. However, if the priests do their duty, the minister, as director and oldest brother, has splendid assistance in the performance of his duties and his public and private acts, and thus his burden will not be too heavy.[62]

This insight reflects the fact that ministry was never intended to be a one-person show. Though some will always serve in leadership or supervisory positions, we all serve as fellow-priests in the Body of Christ. We all have privileges and responsibilities because of our relationship with God through Jesus Christ.

One of the great leaders during America's First Great Awakening was Jonathan Edwards. A brilliant pastor who served his congregation in Northampton in Massachusetts, he was later elected to serve as the president of Princeton University. Based on 1 Peter 2:9—*"But you are a chosen generation, a royal priesthood, a holy nation..."* (NKJV)— Edwards communicated tremendous insights. The following are various excerpts from a message he shared entitled, "Christians a Chosen Generation, a Royal Priesthood, a Holy Nation, A Peculiar People."

> One person, Jesus Christ, is antitype of both kings and priests, under the law. As it is the will of Christ, who became in all things like unto us, that his disciples should in many things become like unto him, so it is in this among others. As Christ is the Son of God, so those that are Christ's are the children of God. As Christ is the heir of God, so as Christ liveth, it is his will that they should live also. As Christ rose from the dead, so it is the will of Christ that his saints should rise also. As Christ is in heaven in glory, so it is the will of Christ that they should be with him where he is. So as Christ is both King and Priest, so shall believers be made kings and priests.[63]

> Jesus Christ is the only proper priest that is to offer sacrifices, and make atonement for sin, under the New Testament. He was the priest of whom all the priests of old were typical. But yet all believers are herein in a measure conformed to their head, and assimilated to him. The priesthood now is no longer confined to one family, to Aaron and his sons, but all the true Israel are priests. Every true Christian has a work and office that is as sacred as that of the priests was under the law, and everyone is advanced to a like honor, and indeed to a greater...

> Every true Christian is allowed as near an access to God, and as free a use of the sacred things, as the priests were of old.

God under the law dwelt in the tabernacle and temple, that were the symbol of his presence, and those places were holy. The seed of Aaron might go into the holy place to minister before the Lord, but if any other came nigh, he was to be put to death, Num. 3:10, "And thou shalt appoint Aaron and his sons, and they shall wait on their priest's office: and the stranger that cometh nigh, shall be put to death."

But now all are allowed to come nigh, we are all allowed a free access to God, to come with boldness and confidence. God's people are not kept at such a distance now as they were under the law…

But now we are all allowed as near an access to God as the high priest only was under the law, and with more freedom, for he might approach but once a year. But Christians may approach boldly at all times through the blood of Christ, without any danger of dying, Heb. 4:16, "Let us, therefore, come boldly unto the throne of grace, that we may obtain mercy, and find grace to help in time of need…"[64]

Christians, by offering obedience to God in their lives and conversation, do what the apostle calls offering their bodies to be a living sacrifice, holy and acceptable to God, as their reasonable service (Rom. 12:1). They offer their bodies, that is they dedicate their bodies to holy uses and purposes. They yield their members as instruments of righteousness unto holiness. The soul, while here, acts externally by the body. And in this Christians serve God. They yield their eyes, their ears, their tongues, their hands, and feet, as servants to God, to be obedient to the dictates of his Word, and of his Holy Spirit in the soul.[65]

It is a great honor to be priests of God. It was a great honor of old to be a priest under the law. It was greater in some respects than to be a king, because they were nearer to God, and they in their work were more immediately concerned with him: it was a more holy and divine office. But more honorable is it to be of the spiritual priesthood. The access to God is nearer, and an infinitely greater privilege…

It would be a dreadful presumption for you to seek this honor if you had not a call to it, Heb. 5:4, "No man taketh this honor unto himself, but he that is called of God, as was Aaron." But you are called, and now it would be presumption and profane contempt in you to refuse it: to refuse such an honor as God offers you…

For direction, that you may be one of this spiritual priest-hood, seek of God his holy anointing, that is that God would pour out his Spirit in his sanctifying influences upon you…

Let all who profess themselves Christians take heed that they do not defile themselves and profane their sacred character. There was great strictness required of old of the priests, lest they should defile themselves and profane their office, and it was regarded as a dreadful thing to profane it. So holy a God hath threatened in the New Testament, that "if any man defile the temple of God, him will God destroy." 1 Cor. 3:17. As Christians are here called the temple of God, so it is said, in the fifth verse , "Ye are a spiritual house, an holy priesthood." Avoid the commission of all immoralities, or things that have a horrid filthiness in them, things that will dreadfully profane the sacred name by which you are called, and the sacred sta-tion wherein you are set…

See that you well execute your office. Offer up your heart in sacrifice. Get and keep a near access to God. Come with bold-ness. Offer up a heart broken for sin; offer it up flaming with love to God; offer praise to God. Praise God for his glorious excellency, and for his love and mercy. Consider what great things you have to praise God for: the redemption of Jesus

Christ, his sufferings, his obedience, and the gift of that holiness, which makes you like unto God.

Be ready to distribute, willing to communicate, and do good. Consider it is part of your office thus to do to which you are called and anointed, and as a sacrifice well-pleasing to God. Pity others in distress and be ready to help one another. God will have mercy and not sacrifice.

And be much in offering up your prayers to God, and see that all your offerings are offered upon the right altar, otherwise they will be abominable to God. Offer your hearts to God through Jesus Christ. In his name present the sacrifice of praise, obedience, charity, and of prayer on the golden altar perfumed with the incense of Christ's merits. Your reward will be to have this honor in heaven, to be exalted to that glorious priesthood, to be made a priest unto God forever and ever.[66]

Charles Spurgeon was another great leader in the history of the church who had a solid grasp on the priesthood of all believers. In a sermon he preached in November of 1874 entitled "The Consecration of Priests," in the early part of the message, Spurgeon asserted:

It is the grand design of all the works of divine grace, both for us and in us, to fit us for the office of the spiritual priesthood, and it will be the crown of our perfection when with all our brethren we shall sing unto the Lord Jesus the new song, "Unto him that loved us, and washed us from our sins in his own blood, and hath made us kings and priests unto God and his Father; to him be glory and dominion for ever and ever." This honor have all the saints: according to Peter, in the second chapter of his First Epistle, it belongs even to newborn babes in grace, for even such are spoken of as forming part of an holy priesthood, to offer up spiritual sacrifices. Nor is this confined to men as was the Aaronic priesthood, for in Christ Jesus there is neither male nor female.[67]

He later challenged all believers to embrace their priestly responsibilities.

I shall ask two questions in closing. Do you and I offer sacrifice continually? Unto this we are called, according to the apostle, that we should offer the sacrifice of prayer and praise continually. To him the cherubim continually cry "Holy, holy, holy." Do we every day feel that our whole being is "Holiness unto the Lord?" In the workshop, in the home, at the fireside, in the field, as well as in the prayer meeting, the vows of God are upon us; we are a separated people, and belong unto God alone? O see ye to this! What have you to offer now? Have you brought an offering now? What will you render unto God for all his benefits towards you? Is there nothing to be done for Christ this afternoon? no sick one to be visited, no poor child to be instructed, no backslider to be reclaimed? Shall a single hour go by without a sacrifice? I charge you, brethren, continually bring of your substance, continually bring of your talent, continually bring of your influence. If God be God, and if you be his priests, serve him. If you be not his ordained ones, then you live unto your-selves, and it will be well to know it: anything is better than to be hypocrites: but if you be true men I beseech you by the mercies of God that ye present your bodies, your souls, your spirits unto God, which is but a reasonable service. When you have once for all made the consecration, may God grant you grace continually to stand to it, and he shall have the glory, for ever and ever. Amen.[68]

In 1855, Spurgeon preached:

Those who are kings and priests are great indeed; and here you behold the saint honored, not with one title, or one office, but with two. He is made not a king merely, but a king and a priest; not a priest merely, but a priest and a king. The saint has two offices conferred upon him at once, he is made a priestly monarch, and a regal priest.[69]

We are priests, because priests are divinely chosen persons, and so are we… We are priests, divinely constituted. All saints are priests… Every saint of the Lord is a priest at God's altar, and is bound to worship God with the holy incense of prayer and praise. We are priests, each one of us, if we are called by divine grace; for thus we are priests by divine constitution.[70]

Then another remark, to finish up with, shall be, we have a divine service to perform; and as I want you all, this morning, to turn this chapel into one great altar—as I want to make you all working priests, and this the temple for sacrifice— look earnestly at your service. You are all priests, because you love his dear name and have a great sacrifice to perform; not a propitiation for your sins, for that has been once offered, but a sacrifice this day of holy thanksgiving. Oh! how sweet in God's ear is the prayer of his people! That is the sacrifice that he accepts; and when their holy hymn swells upwards towards the sky, how pleasant it is in his ears; because then he can say, "My hosts of priests are sacrificing praise."[71]

All of these remarkable statements about the priesthood of all believers were made by amazing church leaders throughout history. When I consider what Justin, Irenaeus, Luther, Calvin, Spener, Edwards, and Spurgeon proclaimed in their day, it makes me wonder how much believers in our generation have recognized and embraced what these men of old saw concerning our shared priesthood. May there be a fresh awakening of these precious truths in our generation as well.

LESSONS FROM THE OLD TESTAMENT PRIESTHOOD

Allow me to introduce you to a priest named Zechariah—not the Old Testament prophet by the same name, but the father of John the Baptist. He and his wife, Elizabeth, lived in the time leading up to and following Jesus' birth. We are going to explore the priesthood through his experience. Early in Luke's Gospel we learn the following:

> When Herod was king of Judea, there was a Jewish priest named Zechariah. He was a member of the priestly order of Abijah, and his wife, Elizabeth, was also from the priestly line of Aaron. Zechariah and Elizabeth were righteous in God's eyes, careful to obey all of the Lord's commandments and regulations. They had no children because Elizabeth was unable to conceive, and they were both very old (Luke 1:5–7 NLT).

Much in the first chapter of Luke is connected to the story of the Nativity, but we will focus instead on the elements that will provide us with a better understanding of the Old Testament priesthood.

In the earliest biblical records, heads of families often served as priests, but as the number of God's people greatly increased, a need for a more formalized priesthood arose. God spoke to Moses about who exactly would step in and fulfill those priestly responsibilities in Israel.

> *Call for your brother, Aaron, and his sons, Nadab, Abihu, Elea-zar, and Ithamar. Set them apart from the rest of the people of Israel so they may minister to me and be my priests* (Exodus 28:1 NLT).

From this point forward, Aaron, his sons, and his future male descen-dants were the priestly line that served God and his people in matters of sacrifices and worship.

Zechariah and his wife were both of priestly lineage—descendants of Aaron—although only the males could serve as priests. Old Testament priests were expected to marry *"virgins of Israel or the widows of the priests."* They were not to *"marry other widows or divorced women"* (Ezekiel 44:22 NLT). Priests could not marry prostitutes or divorced women (see Levit-icus 21:7). We also learn that Zechariah and Elizabeth were devout and sincere in their commitment to God. They respected his holiness and took his commandments very seriously.

As a child, Zechariah's father would have explained to him what an exceptional privilege it was for him to have been born into the priestly line. Only a small percentage of Israel's population could take part in the privileges of the priesthood. Less than five percent of the people served in the priesthood or carried out other responsibilities in caring for Israel's place of worship. If you weren't a male from the right family or the correct tribe, you could not serve as a priest or even assist the priests as the Levites did.

Actually, there were many other restrictions about who could serve in the priesthood. Even if you were a male descendant of Aaron, you could not be a priest if you had any kind of physical defect. That list included blindness, lameness, being disfigured or deformed, having a broken foot or arm, being hunchbacked or dwarfed, having a defective eye, skin sores, scabs, or damaged testicles (see Leviticus 21:18–21).

The Book of Leviticus served as the major source of guidance and information for Zechariah and other Old Testament priests. The introductory remarks for the Book of Leviticus in the New King James Version provide helpful information about Leviticus. For example:

> The Talmud refers to Leviticus as the "Law of the Priests," and the "Law of the Offerings." The Greek title appearing in the Septuagint is *Leuitikon*, "That Which Pertains to the Levites." From this word, the Latin Vulgate derived its name *Leviticus* which was adopted as the English title. This title is slightly misleading because the book does not deal with the Levites as a whole but more with the priests, a segment of the Levites.

Zechariah would not only have been instructed in the technical procedures pertaining to carrying out priestly duties from this book, but he would have also learned what a sacred responsibility it was to be a priest to the Most High God. He must have found it terribly sobering to learn that two of Aaron's sons, Nadab and Abihu, were killed when they offered what the Bible calls strange, profane, or unauthorized fire.

God had very specific guidelines in how Israel was to worship him, and this event that happened early in the priesthood served as a stark reminder that God's standards were not to be trifled with.

> *Then Moses and Aaron went into the Tabernacle, and when they came back out, they blessed the people again, and the glory of the LORD appeared to the whole community. Fire blazed forth from the LORD's presence and consumed the burnt offering and the fat on the altar. When the people saw this, they*

shouted with joy and fell face down on the ground. Aaron's sons
Nadab and Abihu put coals of fire in their incense burners and
sprinkled incense over them. In this way, they disobeyed the
LORD by burning before him the wrong kind of fire, different
than he had commanded. So fire blazed forth from the LORD's
presence and burned them up, and they died there before the
LORD (Leviticus 9:23–10:2 NLT).

When we read that Zechariah and his wife were *"careful to obey all*
of the Lord's commandments and regulations" (Luke 1:6 NLT), we can
appreciate that wise priests and wise Israelites in general had learned to
reverentially fear God and honor his holiness.

However, not everyone respected God or his commandments. Zechariah would also have learned about priests from previous centuries who
had been corrupt, such as the sons of Eli, Hophni and Phinehas (see 1
Samuel 2:12). God said at yet another time, *"Your priests have violated my*
instructions and defiled my holy things..." (Ezekiel 22:26 NLT).

By the time of Malachi, the last of the Old Testament prophets, God
said that the priests had dishonored and shown contempt for his name
(see Malachi 1:6,12 NLT). The deterioration that had taken place by the
end of the Old Testament was such that God also said:

"For the lips of a priest should keep knowledge, and people should
seek the law from his mouth; for he is the messenger of the LORD
of hosts. But you have departed from the way; you have caused
many to stumble at the law. You have corrupted the covenant of
Levi," says the LORD of hosts (Malachi 2:7–8 NKJV).

Zechariah would likely not have lived to see it, but priests would later
get a bad rap because, as the New Testament records, the chief priests
conspired and aggressively pushed for Jesus' crucifixion. Zechariah's life,

though, reminds us that there were good and godly men who also served as priests, and I'm sure there were others who shared his sincerity.

It is easy, though, to single out and pick on the evil, corrupt, disobedient priests of the Old Testament. We need to remember that not only were they unregenerate—the New Birth was not available until after Jesus died and rose again—but also that there have always been bad apples in every barrel. There have been corrupt bankers, lawyers, teachers, businessmen, and yes, preachers. The reason the entire system was set up is because people without God are sinful, fallen, and in desperate need of salvation and forgiveness. Though the people involved were imperfect, we must not forget what was behind the structure of the sacrifices.

The entire sacrificial system of the Old Testament was designed to point people toward God's mercy and to foreshadow the Ultimate Sacrifice who would be offered for the sins of all humanity—the Lord Jesus Christ. The death of the various sacrificial animals in the Old Testament and the shedding of blood spoke to the fact that sin is serious and must be judged. The fact that a substitute could take the place of the guilty party and that forgiveness could be extended spoke of God's tremendous love and mercy for the sinner. Priests were responsible to carry out these sacrifices God's way to paint a true picture of God's plan of redemption.

THE CONSECRATION OF PRIESTS

Before Zechariah could have actually begun serving as a priest, he would have gone through a special consecration or ordination service. Exodus 29:20 describes how Aaron and his sons were set apart—the blood of a sacrificial animal was placed on their right earlobe, the thumb of their right hand, and the big toe of their right feet. This symbolized their consecration to God. All that they heard was to be "through the blood." In other words, they were to listen to God completely with hearts of obedience. Also consecrated to God was the work of their hands (symbolized by the blood on their right thumb), along with their walk or their lifestyle (symbolized by the blood on their right big toe).

The priests were directed to repeat a similar process when people sought ceremonial cleansing. Not only would the priest apply the blood to the earlobe, right thumb, and right big toe of the inquirer, but he would then:

> *Apply some of the oil in his palm over the blood from the guilt offering that is on the lobe of the right ear, the thumb of the right hand, and the big toe of the right foot of the person being purified* (Leviticus 14:17 NLT).

God seemed to be sending a very strong message—he wants our hearing, our work, and our walk cleansed by the blood and anointed by the Spirit.

What Did the Priests Do?

One commentary describes the role of priests in the Old Testament:

> In their sanctuary service the priests were charged with maintaining holiness. They alone were to tend to the golden incense altar, the lamps, the Bread of the Presence, and the altar of sacrifice. But the primary role of a priest was that of a mediator representing God before mankind, and mankind before God.[72]

As the nation grew and as the number of priests increased, it was necessary for there to be a "head"—known as the high priest—to lead and

organize the entire system. Aaron was the first one to stand in this particular office, and when he died, his son Eleazar took his place.

While the priests would offer daily sacrifices, the high priest alone
would go into the Holy of Holies once a year on the Day of Atonement
and stand before the mercy seat. There, on behalf of the entire nation, he
would secure God's forgiveness for the people. Because he represented
all of Israel, the high priest wore a special breastplate with twelve stones,
representing the twelve tribes. In his priestly function, he not only represented the people before God, but also represented God to the people.

We gain some insight into the role and the function of the regular
priests in what Luke wrote about Zechariah, the father of John the Baptist.

> One day Zechariah was serving God in the Temple, for his
> order was on duty that week. As was the custom of the priests,
> he was chosen by lot to enter the sanctuary of the Lord and
> burn incense. While the incense was being burned, a great
> crowd stood outside, praying (Luke 1:8–10 NLT).

This passage references the order of priests to which Zechariah belonged;
it was that of Abijah (see Luke 1:5), one of twenty-four different divisions
of priests in Israel. There were approximately 18,000 priests at that time,
which necessitated them being divided into orders or divisions. Each order
would only serve two weeks out of the year; in addition, all of the priests
would serve during the Feasts of Passover, Pentecost, and Tabernacles.

The priests would carry out various duties during their assigned times
in Jerusalem, but a large number of them would never have the privilege
of entering into the Holy Place to offer incense to God. There were so
many priests that those who were fortunate enough to be chosen by lot
could enter the Holy Place only once in their entire lifetime. Noted com-
mentator, William Barclay, writes:

Every morning and evening sacrifice was made for the whole nation. A burnt offering of a male lamb, one year old, without spot or blemish was offered, together with a meat offering of flour and oil and a drink offering of wine. Before the morning sacrifice and after the evening sacrifice incense was burned on the altar of incense so that, as it were, the sacrifices might go up to God wrapped in an envelope of sweet-smelling incense. It was quite possible that many a priest would never have the privilege of burning incense all his life; but if the lot did fall on any priest that day was the greatest day in all his life, the day he longed for and dreamed of. On this day the lot fell on Zacharias and he would be thrilled to the core of his being.[73]

Though Zechariah was *"very old"* (Luke 1:7 NLT), this would be the first and the last time that he would be privileged to enter the Holy Place.

TOUCHING ALL THE BASES

More than forty years ago, I read a delightful book about the Old Testament priests with a specific focus on their garments. The author, C. W. Slemming made the following observations about priests. I believe it is worth repeating here. He asserted that the priests were:

- Called (see Exodus 28:1; Hebrews 5:4)

- Cleansed (see Exodus 29:4)

- Clothed (see Exodus 29:5,8)

- Consecrated (see Exodus 29:7,20,44–46)

- Compassionate (see Hebrews 4:14–15; 5:1–3)

- Commissioned

Regarding that last point—Commissioned—Slemming writes:

> Their commission is to be found throughout the book of Levit-
> icus. They had to obey all the instructions of the Lord God
> and to become, through the sacrifices, intercessors between
> God and man. Christ today is fulfilling His priestly functions
> on our behalf, and as His children we must fulfill ours.[74]

Do you think that many believers today have any idea how privileged they are as priests under the new covenant? Zechariah only got to go into the Holy Place once in his entire lifetime; most of his colleagues never had that opportunity. Because of Jesus, we are a holy and a royal priesthood (see 1 Peter 2:5,9), and we have the privilege to not only enter, but to live in the presence of God. The author of Hebrews tells us, *"And so, dear brothers and sisters, we can boldly enter heaven's Most Holy Place because of the blood of Jesus"* (Hebrews 10:19 NLT).

Do you remember what the regular, common people were doing while Zechariah was offering up incense in the Holy Place? *"While the incense was being burned, a great crowd stood outside, praying"* (Luke 1:10 NLT). No doubt that was meaningful to them as they awaited the priest to come out and bless them. But they still had to stand *outside* the Temple while one priest went *in.* Today, every single believer in Jesus Christ is beckoned and encouraged,

> *Let us go right into the presence of God with sincere hearts fully*
> *trusting him. For our guilty consciences have been sprinkled*
> *with Christ's blood to make us clean, and our bodies have been*
> *washed with pure water* (Hebrews 10:22 NLT).

This invitation is not just for the male descendants of Aaron. It is for every born-again child of God. We have the privilege of access to God, and we have responsibilities as we live our lives in relationship to one another.

THE OLD PRIESTHOOD WAS NEVER MEANT TO BE PERMANENT

A careful reading of the Book of Hebrews reveals that the Aaronic priest-hood of the Old Testament was never meant to be permanent. Jesus Christ would come and fulfill all of the requirements of the old covenant and inaugurate *"a far better covenant with God, based on better promises"* (Hebrews 8:6 NLT). Volumes have been written contrasting the old and new covenants, but let's look at a few key verses from Hebrews to under-stand how things are different today and why that old priesthood has ceased.

> *...It was necessary for him* [Jesus] *to be made in every respect like us, his brothers and sisters, so that he could be our merci-ful and faithful High Priest before God. Then he could offer a sacrifice that would take away the sins of the people* (Hebrews 2:17 NLT).

> *So then, since we have a great High Priest who has entered heaven, Jesus the Son of God, let us hold firmly to what we believe* (Hebrews 4:14 NLT).

> *...He* [Jesus] *has become our eternal High Priest in the order of Melchizedek* (Hebrews 6:20 NLT).

> *So if the priesthood of Levi, on which the law was based, could have achieved the perfection God intended, why did God need to establish a different priesthood, with a priest in the order of Melchizedek instead of the order of Levi and Aaron?* (Hebrews 7:11 NLT).

Jesus became a priest, not by meeting the physical requirement of belonging to the tribe of Levi, but by the power of a life that cannot be destroyed (Hebrews 7:16 NLT).

There were many priests under the old system, for death prevented them from remaining in office. But because Jesus lives forever, his priesthood lasts forever (Hebrews 7:23–24 NLT).

Unlike those other high priests, he [Jesus] *does not need to offer sacrifices every day. They did this for their own sins first and then for the sins of the people. But Jesus did this once for all when he offered himself as the sacrifice for the people's sins* (Hebrews 7:27 NLT).

The Book of Hebrews provides many other vital insights about Christ fulfilling the old covenant and instituting this new covenant, of which we partake. A detailed study of that powerful New Testament book will always prove beneficial. Hopefully, though, the verses cited above will help us begin thinking about Christ's supremacy and the impact of his high priesthood over all of our lives.

We must never forget this fact: Because he is our High Priest, all believers now comprise a holy priesthood, a royal priesthood, and we are all kings and priests unto God our Father (see 1 Peter 2:5,9; Revelation 1:6 NKJV). Peter and John emphatically declared this truth, and Paul alluded to it various times as we noted in Chapter Two.

The Old Testament Tabernacle and Temple served their purpose in their time. The author of Hebrews referred to the old system with its sacrifices and rituals as a *"system of worship that is only a copy, a shadow of the real one in heaven"* (Hebrews 8:5 NLT) and proceeded to say,

But now Jesus, our High Priest, has been given a ministry that is far superior to the old priesthood, for he is the one who mediates for us a far better covenant with God, based on better promises. If the first covenant had been faultless, there would have been no need for a second covenant to replace it (Hebrews 8:6–7 NLT).

Aaron and his successors were the high priests of that old system, but Jesus is the High Priest of the new covenant.

The Lord Jesus will have no successors, but he does have a myriad of priests serving under him. Who are those priests? We are! The priests who now serve under him include every blood-bought, blood-washed child of God. Under the old system, only the priests could blow the trumpet (see Numbers 10:8), but every child of God today is called to be part of expressing the joyful sound! Paul told the entire Philippian church to be *"blameless and harmless, children of God without fault in the midst of a crooked and perverse generation, among whom you shine as lights in the world, holding fast the word of life..."* (Philippians 2:15–16 NKJV).

WHO WERE THE LEVITES, AND WHAT DID THEY DO?

Aaron and Moses were of the tribe of Levi, the third son of Jacob and Leah. While only the descendants of Aaron could serve as priests, other members of the tribe of Levi (known as the Levites) would assist the priests in various matters, especially in caring for the Tabernacle and the Temple. We might say it this way: All priests were Levites, but not all Levites were priests.

When the Israelites rebelled against God and engaged in great wickedness in the golden calf incident, Moses issued a challenge:

> So he [Moses] *stood at the entrance to the camp and shouted,*
> *"All of you who are on the LORD's side, come here and join me."*
> *And all the Levites gathered around him* (Exodus 32:26 NLT).

Because the Levites had risen to this challenge at a critical time in Israel's history, God designated this tribe—the tribe of Levi—to become the caretakers of Israel's place of worship. The Tabernacle was a portable tent structure where sacrifices were made during the Israelites' wanderings through the wilderness.

The Tabernacle remained the place of Israel's worship until the Temple—a more permanent and stationary facility—was built under Solomon. I use the word *permanent* loosely because the Temple was destroyed by the Babylonians, rebuilt under Zerubbabel (see the Book of Ezra), reconstructed under King Herod, and finally demolished by the Romans in AD 70.

The Levites worked in and around the Tabernacle but did not engage in the priestly duties. Here is a description of their charge:

> *Put the Levites in charge of the Tabernacle of the Covenant, along with all its furnishings and equipment. They must carry the Tabernacle and all its furnishings as you travel, and they must take care of it and camp around it. Whenever it is time for the Tabernacle to move, the Levites will take it down. And when it is time to stop, they will set it up again. But any unauthorized person who goes too near the Tabernacle must be put to death. Each tribe of Israel will camp in a designated area with its own family banner. But the Levites will camp around the Tabernacle of the Covenant to protect the community of Israel from the LORD's anger. The Levites are responsible to stand guard around the Tabernacle* (Numbers 1:50–53 NLT).

The Levites engaged in manual labor relative to the Tabernacle as Israel traveled, setting it up and dismantling it as need required and transporting all of its furnishings and equipment. In this sense, the Levites served in the ministry of helps in all things relative to the Tabernacle and, later, to the Temple.

God specifically told Aaron that he and his sons would be responsible for matters of the priesthood, and then said, *"I myself have chosen your fellow Levites from among the Israelites to be your special assistants. They are a gift to you, dedicated to the LORD for service in the Tabernacle"* (Numbers

18:6 NLT). So, from one tribe of Israel, God selected certain men—priests (Aaron and his descendants) who would stand as mediators between God and the people and the Levites who would be their helpers.

Nothing Haphazard

We see in various places throughout Scripture that God specializes in order and efficiency (e.g. Creation, Moses' helpers in Exodus 18:13–26, those who assisted the apostles in Acts 6:1–7). The same type of thorough and systematic arrangement is found in how the Levites engaged in their respective assignments with the Tabernacle and later with the Temple.

Meticulous attention was given to which families within the Levitical tribe would be responsible for which parts of the Tabernacle. For example:

- The Gershonites *"were responsible to care for the Tabernacle, including the sacred tent with its layers of coverings, the curtain at its entrance, the curtains of the courtyard that surrounded the Tabernacle and altar, the curtain at the courtyard entrance, the ropes, and all the equipment related to their use"* (Numbers 3:25–26 NLT).

- The Kohathites *"were responsible for the care of the sanctuary"* which included *"the Ark, the table, the lampstand, the altars, the various articles used in the sanctuary, the inner curtain, and all the equipment related to their use"* (Numbers 3:28,30–31 NLT).

- The Merarites *"were responsible for the care of the frames supporting the Tabernacle, the crossbars, the pillars, the bases, and all the equipment related to their use. They were also*

> *responsible for the posts of the courtyard and all their bases,*
> *pegs, and ropes"* (Numbers 3:36–37 NLT).

As you continue reading in the Book of Numbers, you find out that all of the priest and Levites had distinct responsibilities. Nothing was left to chance. There were clear lines of communication, responsibility, and accountability.

After Israel settled in the Promised Land, the Tabernacle was not being moved from place to place, but the Levites still had many responsibilities. About David's final days, we read:

> *All the Levites who were thirty years old or older were counted,*
> *and the total came to 38,000. Then David said, "From all the*
> *Levites, 24,000 will supervise the work at the Temple of the*
> *LORD. Another 6,000 will serve as officials and judges. Another*
> *4,000 will work as gatekeepers, and 4,000 will praise the LORD*
> *with the musical instruments I have made"* (1 Chronicles 23:3–5 NLT).

Some may find this information outdated and irrelevant, but I find it fascinating. Why? Even though we are no longer under the Levitical system of the Old Testament, we know that God wants everyone to have a sense of purpose and to engage in meaningful work.

Even though only a small portion of God's people in the Old Testament qualified to serve him in the ways we have been exploring, every New Testament believer has the privilege of serving God and being part of this wonderful priesthood that the New Testament so clearly and beautifully presents. As stated in the second chapter, our priesthood means that we have both the privilege of accessing the presence and blessings of God, as well as the responsibility of sharing and conveying those blessings with others.

APPENDIX D

ONE ANOTHER

In case you have not yet identified your specific gifts, calling, or assignment from God, don't worry. God has plenty of general instructions for all of us, and if we apply ourselves to putting the following admonitions into practice, we'll all stay plenty busy. The following bullet list is borrowed from my book, *Relationships Matter: Lessons from Paul and the People Who Impacted His Life.*[75]

God values our relationships so highly that the words *one another* are used repeatedly throughout the New Testament. Consider how these dynamic words are used in Scripture:

- *Have peace with one another* (Mark 9:50 NKJV).

- *Love one another* (John 13:34–35; 15:12,17 NKJV).

- *We are members of one another* (Romans 12:5 NKJV).

- *In honor prefer one another* (Romans 12:10 NKJV).

- *Edify one another* (Romans 14:19 NKJV).

- *Be like-minded toward one another* (Romans 15:5 NKJV).

- *Receive one another* (Romans 15:7 NKJV).

- *Admonish one another* (Romans 15:14 NKJV).

- *Learn to be considerate of one another* (1 Corinthians 1:10 MSG).

- *Be reverent and courteous with one another* (1 Corinthians 11:33 MSG).

- *Care for one another* (1 Corinthians 12:25 NKJV).

- *Serve one another* (Galatians 5:13 NKJV).

- *Bear one another's burdens* (Galatians 6:2 NKJV).

- *Bearing with one another in love* (Ephesians 4:2 NKJV).

- *Be kind to one another, tenderhearted, forgiving one another* (Ephesians 4:32 NKJV).

- *Submitting to one another* (Ephesians 5:21 NKJV).

- *Instruct and direct one another* (Colossians 3:16 MSG).

- *Increase and abound in love to one another* (1 Thessalonians 3:12 NKJV).

- *Comfort one another* (1 Thessalonians 4:18 NKJV).

- *Comfort each other and edify one another* (1 Thessalonians 5:11 NKJV).

- *Always pursue what is good for one another* (1 Thessalonians 5:15 NET).

- *Motivate one another to acts of love and good works and encourage one another* (Hebrews 10:24-25 NLT).

- *Be on the watch to look after one another* (Hebrews 12:15 AMPC).

- *Confess your trespasses to one another, and pray for one another, that you may be healed* (James 5:16 NKJV).

- *Having compassion for one another* (1 Peter 3:8 NKJV).

- *Be hospitable to one another* (1 Peter 4:9 NKJV).

- *Be submissive to one another* (1 Peter 5:5 NKJV).

- *We have fellowship with one another* (1 John 1:7 NKJV).

It is not surprising that both Peter and Paul taught believers to *"love one another"* (1 Thessalonians 4:9; 1 Peter 1:22), and John repeated the same admonition multiple times (see 1 John 3:11,23; 4:7,11–12; 2 John 5).

Imagine what a difference it would make if every believer would make a conscious, deliberate effort to specifically act on and implement just three of these admonitions every day? What a difference it would make in the quality of our relationships and in the level of love and care expressed among believers. Even if you think you stand in some lofty spiritual office, you are not exempt from these. Remember, these are basic Christian responsibilities in which all of us should regularly engage.

THE PRAYER OF SALVATION

God loves you—no matter who you are, no matter what is in your past. God loves you so much that he gave his one and only begotten Son for you. Even though all of us have sinned (see Romans 3:23), the Bible tells us that *"whoever believes in him shall not perish but have eternal life"* (John 3:16 NIV). Jesus laid down his life and rose again so that we could not only spend eternity with him in Heaven, but so that we could also have a vibrant relationship with him in the here and now. If you would like to make Jesus the Lord of your life, say the following prayer out loud and mean it from your heart.

> *Dear Heavenly Father,*
>
> *I thank you that Jesus died for my sins on the cross, that he shed his blood for my forgiveness, and that he was raised from the dead so that I could come into right relationship with you.*
>
> *Your word says that if I come to you, you will never cast me out (John 6:37), so I know you won't reject me, but you receive and accept me, and I thank you for it.*
>
> *You said in your word that if I call upon the name of the Lord, I will be saved (Romans 10:13). I am calling on your name right now, so I thank you for saving me.*

You also said that if I will confess with my mouth that Jesus is Lord and believe with my heart that God raised him from the dead, I will be saved (Romans 10:9). Jesus, I confess you right now as my Lord. I turn away from my old life, and I surrender all that I am to you.

You are alive, and I accept the forgiveness, the mercy, and the new life that you are offering me now. Thank you for helping me to live for you all the days of my life. Amen.

Now What?

Praying as you just prayed is a lot like an introduction at the beginning of a relationship. God doesn't intend for you to greet and accept him through such a prayer and then go on with the rest of your life as though you'd never met him. He desires a growing relationship with you in which you come to know him more and more and grow in your faith and fellowship with him. In other words, what you did in praying that prayer was not a last step, but a first step.

Below are some important steps to move forward in your relationship with God:

1. **Get a Bible and begin reading it.** I suggest you begin by reading the Gospel of John followed by the Book of Romans. Many good translations of the Bible exist; I suggest you use one that is easy for you to understand. The New Living Translation is a good choice.

2. **Find a good church and attend regularly.** It is important to become a part of a church that believes in the lordship of

Jesus, the authority of the Bible, and the power of the Holy Spirit. Your spiritual walk and your spiritual growth will be greatly helped by your involvement in a good church.

3. **Get baptized** (see Matthew 28:19). Water Baptism is your public declaration that you have left your old life behind and have begun a new life in Christ. In addition to being baptized in water, ask God to fill you with the Holy Spirit. The Holy Spirit already lives in you if you have accepted Jesus as your Savior, but there is an additional experience by which He fills you with power. In the Bible, you can read all about the outstanding works of the Holy Spirit in the Book of Acts.

4. **Pray.** Prayer involves both listening to and talking with God. You don't have to use fancy or religious-sounding words when you talk to God. As you learn more and more about the Bible, you'll know better how to speak God's "language," but you can always talk to God from your heart and ask him to help you in everything.

5. **Tell others.** What has happened in your life is a great thing! You have passed from spiritual death to spiritual life. Pray about who God might have you share your good news with. The world is full of hurting people who need to know about God's love and what Jesus can do for them.

NOTES

1. Charles H. Spurgeon, "Belief, Baptism, Blessing" in *The Metropolitan Tabernacle Pulpit*, Volume XXXVIII, 1892, Sermon 2275 (Pasadena, TX: Pilgrim Publications), 463–464.

2. See Appendix D, One Another.

3. Kenneth E. Hagin, *He Gave Gifts Unto Men: A Biblical Perspective of Apostles, Prophets, and Pastors,* Kindle edition (Tulsa, OK: Faith Library Publications, 1992), 1180.

4. Charles Spurgeon, "The Kingly Priesthood of the Saints" in *The New Park Street Pulpit: Containing Sermons Preached by Revised by the Rev. C. H. Spurgeon*, Volume 1, January 28, 1855 (Pasadena, TX: Pilgrim Publications, 1975), 70.

5. Jonathan Edwards, "Christians a chosen Generation, a royal Priesthood, a holy Nation, a peculiar People" *in The Works of Jonathan Edwards, Volume 2* (Edinburgh, UK: The Banner of Truth Trust, 1974), 943.

6. C. S. Lewis, *The Weight of Glory*, Preached originally as a sermon on June 8, 1942: published in THEOLOGY, November, 1941, and by the S.P.C.K, 1942.

7. A. W. Tozer, *That Incredible Christian: How Heaven's Children Live on Earth,* Kindle edition (Camp Hill, PA: Wing Spread Publishers, 2008), 1477.

8. Henry Blackaby and Tom Blackaby, *Anointed to Be God's Servants: Lessons from the Life of Paul and His Companions* (Nashville: Thomas Nelson, 2005), 149–150.

9. A. W. Tozer, *Tragedy in the Church: The Missing Gifts,* Kindle edition (Chicago: First Moody Publishers, 1990), 13.

10. Billy Graham, *Just As I Am: The Autobiography of Billy Graha*m, Kindle edition (New York: HarperCollins Publishers, 1997), 670.

11. Many modern translations render this word *encouraging* as opposed to *exhortation.*

12. Walter A. Elwell and Philip Wesley Comfort, *Tyndale Bible Dictionary*, Tyndale Reference Library (Wheaton, IL: Tyndale House Publishers, 2001), 453.

13. Taken from *Giving it All Away… And Getting it All Back Again: The Way of Living Generously*, Kindle edition, by David Green. Copyright © 2017.   Used by permission of HarperCollins Christian Publishing. www.harpercollinschristian.com

14. Ibid.

15. Ibid.

16. Henry Blackaby and Tom Blackaby, *Anointed to be God's Servants: How God Blesses Those Who Serve Together,* Kindle edition (Nashville: Thomas Nelson Publishers, 2005), 93–94.

17. A. W. Tozer, *Tragedy in the Church: The Missing Gifts,* Kindle edition (Chicago: Moody Publishers, 1990), 15.

18. Peter Wagner, *Your Spiritual Gifts Can Help Your Church Grow,* Kindle edition (Bloomington, MN: Chosen Books, 2017), 391.

19. Charles H. Spurgeon, "A New Order of Priests and Levites" in *The Metropolitan Tabernacle Pulpit,* Volume XVII, Sermon 992 (Pasadena, TX: Pilgrim Publications), 293.

20. Charles Spurgeon, *Only a Prayer Meeting,* Kindle edition (Dublin: Cooper Publications, 2020), 137.

21. Ibid., 138.

22. Ibid., 7.

23. Charles H. Spurgeon, "Prayer for the Church" in *The Metropolitan Tabernacle Pulpit,* Volume XLVIII, Sermon 2788 (Pasadena, TX: Pilgrim Publications), 346–347.

24. Charles Spurgeon, *Only a Prayer Meeting,* Kindle edition (Dublin: Cooper Publications, 2020), 138.

25. Charles Finney, *Autobiography of Charles Finney,* Kindle edition (Christian Classic Treasury), 1927.

26. Ibid., 3997.

27. Ibid.

28. Charles E. Hambrick-Stowe, *Charles G. Finney and the Spirit of American Evangelicalism,* Kindle edition (Grand Rapids: William B. Eerdmans Publishing Company, 1966), 1563.

29. Charles Finney, *Autobiography of Charles Finney,* Kindle edition (Christian Classic Treasury), 1000, 4009, 1664, 1827.

30. Ibid., 1661.

31. Ibid., 3994.

32. Andrew Murray, *Believing Prayer,* Kindle edition (Minneapolis: Bethany House Publishers, 2012), 315.

33. Andrew Murray, *The Spiritual Life: Undeniable Ways to Conquer the Flesh and Grow in Christ,* Kindle edition (Apollo, PA: Ichthus Publications, 2015), 63.

34. W. B. Godbey, *Commentary on the New Testament*, Volume IV, Corinthians-Galatians; cited at https://www.studylight.org/commentaries/eng/ges/1-corinthians-12.html.

35. Andrew Murray, *Working for God,* Kindle edition (Abbotsford, WI: Aneko Press, 1901), 16.

36. Donald Gee, *The Ministry Gifts of Christ* (Springfield, MO: Gospel Publishing House, 1930), 19.

37. Donald Gee, *The Ministry Gifts of Christ* (Springfield, MO: Gospel Publishing House, 1930), 21–25.

38. A. B. Simpson, "Aggressive Christianity" *in The Articles and Sermons of A. B. Simpson*, Kindle edition, 3037.

39. Warren's listing includes "warmer through fellowship, deeper through discipleship, stronger through worship, broader through ministry, and larger through evangelism."

40. "Rick Warren: What I Learned from Billy Graham," *Christianity Today;* https://www.christianitytoday.com/ct/2018/billy-graham/rick-warren-what-i-learned-from-billy-graham.html.

41. A. W. Tozer, *The Knowledge of the Holy: The Attributes of God: Their Meaning in the Christian Life* (New York: Harper and Brothers, 1961), 12.

42. Billy Graham, *The Jesus Generation* (Grand Rapids: Zondervan, 1971), 166.

43. Barna Group, "51% of Churchgoers Don't Know of the Great Commission," *Barna* (March 27, 2018); https://www.barna.com/research/half-churchgoers-not-heard-great-commission.

44. See also, Acts 1:22; 2:32; 3:15; 5:32; 10:39, 41; 13:31; 22:15, 20; 26:16.

45. R. C. H. Lenski, *The Interpretation of St. John's Gospel* (Minneapolis, MN: Augsburg Publishing House, 1961), 961.

46. Justin Martyr, *The First Apology of Justin*, Chapter XIV.

47. Tertullian, *The Apology of Tertullian*, Chapter XXXIX.

48. Philip Schaff, *History of the Christian Church*, Volume II (Grand Rapids: Eerdmans, 1910), 375–376.

49. Tony Cooke, *In Search of Timothy: Discovering and Developing Greatness in Church Staff and Volunteers* (Tulsa, OK: Faith Library Publications, 2005), 241.

50. Kennedy Institute of Ethics at Georgetown University, Bioethics Blog, "Death Rate is 120 Per Minute" (accessed June 9, 2022); https://bioethics.georgetown.edu/2016/04/death-rate-is-120-per-minute/.

51. Justin Martyr, *Dialogue of Justin with a Jew*, Chapter CXVI.

52. Irenaeus, *Against Heresies*, Book V, Chapter XXXIV.

53. Martin Luther. *Concerning the Ministry: To the Illustrious Senate and People of Prague*, 1523.

54. Ibid.

55. Martin Luther, *Concerning Christian Liberty*, 1520.

56. "First Sunday after Epiphany," *The Complete Sermons of Martin Luther*, vol. IV (Grand Rapids, MI: Baker Books, 2007), 9.

57. John Calvin, *Institutes of the Christian Religion, Volume 1* (Philadelphia: Westminster Press, 1960), 502.

58. Ibid.

59. John Calvin, *Institutes of the Christian Religion, Volume 2* (Philadelphia: Westminster Press, 1960), 1476.

60. Philip Spener, *Pia Desideria*, Kindle edition (1675), 1590.

61. Ibid.

62. Ibid.

63. Jonathan Edwards, "Christians a chosen Generation, a royal Priesthood, a holy Nation, a peculiar People" in *The Works of Jonathan Edwards*, Volume 2 (Edinburgh, UK: The Banner of Truth Trust, 1974), 940.

64. Ibid., 942.

65. Ibid., 943.

66. Ibid., 944.

67. Charles H. Spurgeon, "The Consecration of Priests" in *The Metropolitan Tabernacle Pulpit*, Volume XX, 1874, Sermon 1203 (Pasadena, TX: Pilgrim Publications), 637.

68. Ibid., 648.

69. Charles Spurgeon, "The Kingly Priesthood of the Saints" in *The New Park Street Pulpit: Containing Sermons Preached by*

Revised by the Rev. C. H. Spurgeon, Volume 1, January 28, 1855 (Pasadena, TX: Pilgrim Publications, 1975), 72.

70. Ibid., 74–75.

71. Ibid., 75.

72. Allen C. Myers, *The Eerdmans Bible Dictionary* (Grand Rapids, MI: Eerdmans, 1987), 849.

73. William Barclay, ed., *The Gospel of Luke*, The Daily Study Bible Series (Philadelphia, PA: The Westminster John Knox Press, 1975), 9–11.

74. C. W. Slemming, *These Are the Garments: A Study of the High Priest's Garments* (Fort Washington, PA: Christian Literature Crusade, 1955), 17.

75. Tony Cooke, *Relationships Matter: Lessons from Paul and the People Who Impacted His Life* (Tulsa, OK: Tony Cooke Ministries, 2020).

ABOUT TONY COOKE

Bible teacher Tony Cooke graduated from RHEMA Bible Training Center in 1980, studied religion at Butler University, received a bachelor's in church ministries from North Central University, and a master's in theological studies/church history from Liberty University. Tony has traveled to more than thirty nations and nearly all fifty states teaching the Bible. He has authored more than a dozen books, many of which are translated into several other languages. Tony and his wife, Lisa, reside in Broken Arrow, Oklahoma.

www.tonycooke.org

Equipping Believers to Walk in the Abundant Life
John 10:10b

Connect with us for fresh content and news about forthcoming books from your favorite authors...

 Facebook @ HarrisonHousePublishers

 Instagram @ HarrisonHousePublishing

 www.harrisonhouse.com